Contemporary

Foundations

Social Studies

Mc Graw Hill **Wright Group**

The McGraw·Hill Companies

www.WrightGroup.com

Send all inquiries to:
Wright Group/McGraw-Hill
P.O. Box 812960
Chicago, IL 60681

ISBN: 978-1-4045-7635-3
MHID: 1-4045-7635-5

2 3 4 5 6 7 8 9 10 11 COU 12 11 10 09

CONTENTS

Contents

ACKNOWLEDGMENTS

Photo on cover, © Christine Balderas/iStock International Inc.

Photo on page 2, © Amy Nichole Harris/Shutterstock Images, LLC

Photo on page 4, © Gideon Mendel/ActionAid/Corbis

Photo on page 6, © North Wind/North Wind Picture Archives

Photo on page 8, © North Wind/North Wind Picture Archives

Photo on page 10, © Holger Mette/Shutterstock Images, LLC

Photo on page 12, Courtesy of © the Winterton Collection of East African Photographs, the Melville J. Herskovits Library of African Studies, Northwestern University

Photo on page 14, © Oleg Nikishin/Stringer/Getty Images

Photo on page 16, © Jean Heguy/First Light/Getty Images

Photo on page 18, © Stapleton Collection/Corbis

Photo on page 20, © 2008 The Associated Press

Photo on page 22, © North Wind/North Wind Picture Archives

Photo on page 24, © AA World Travel Library/Alamy

Photo on page 26, © Mary Evans Picture Library

Photo on page 28, © Peter Leibing/Reuters/AKG Images

Photo on page 30, © Per-Anders Pettersson/Getty Images

Photo on page 32, © The Bridgeman Art Library/Getty Images

Photo on page 34, © Paris Pierce/Alamy

Photo on page 36, © Robert Knopes/omniphoto

Photo on page 38, © iStock International, Inc.

Photo on page 43(l), © Library of Congress, Prints and Photographs Division

Photo on page 43(r), © Library of Congress, Prints and Photographs Division

Photo on page 44, © J. McPhail/Shutterstock Images, LLC

Photo on page 46, © 2008 The Associated Press

Photo on page 49, © Courtesy National Weather Service

Photo on page 50, © The Hulton Archive/Getty Images

Photo on page 52, © Library of Congress, Prints and Photographs Division

Photo on page 54, © Time & Life Pictures/Stringer/Getty Images

Photo on page 56, © 2008 The Associated Press

Photo on page 58, © 2008 The Associated Press

Photo on page 62, © 2008 The Associated Press

Photo on page 64, © Bettmann/Corbis

Photo on page 67(l), © 2008 The Associated Press

Photo on page 67(r), © 2008 The Associated Press

Cartoon on page 69, AUTH © 1986 The Philadelphia Inquirer. Reprinted with permission of UNIVERSAL PRESS SYNDICATE. All rights reserved.

Photo on page 70(t), © 2008 The Associated Press

Photo on page 70(b), © Library of Congress, Prints and Photographs Division

Photo on page 74, © AFP/Getty Images

Photo on page 76, © Jonathan Larsen/Shutterstock Images, LLC

Photo on page 78, © Bettmann/Corbis

Photo on page 85, © Stockbyte/Alamy

Photo on page 86, © 2008 The Associated Press

Photo on page 88, © Digital Vision/Punchstock

Photo on page 92, © Frontpage/Shutterstock Images, LLC

Photo on page 94, © Time & Life Pictures/Getty Images

Photo on page 96, © 2008 The Associated Press

Photo on page 98, © U.S. Army Aviation and Missile Command

Cartoon on page 100, by John Stampone

Cartoon on page 102, Ed Fischer, 1991, Rochester Post-Bulletin. Reprinted with permission of Ed Fischer, www.edfischer.com.

Cartoon on page 104, R. J. Matson, *St. Louis Post Dispatch*, April 3, 2007. Reprinted with permission of the St. Louis Post-Dispatch, copyright 2007.

Cartoon on page 106, (c) 2007 TAB, *The Calgary Sun* and PoliticalCartoons.com. Used by permission.

Cartoon on page 109, (c) 2009 Pat Bagley, *Salt Lake Tribune* and PoliticalCartoons. com. Used by permission.

Photo on page 110, © Hulton Archives/Getty Images

Photo on page 138, © TWPhoto/Corbis

Cartoon on page 175, Jeff Parker, *FLORIDA TODAY.* Used by permission.

The editor has made every effort to trace ownership of all copyrighted material and to secure the necessary permissions. Should there be a question regarding the use of any material, regret is hereby expressed for such error. Upon notification of any such oversight, proper acknowledgment will be made in future editions.

Introduction

Welcome to Contemporary's *Foundations: Social Studies*. This book will help you understand social studies texts. You will practice reading social studies passages and writing about social studies topics.

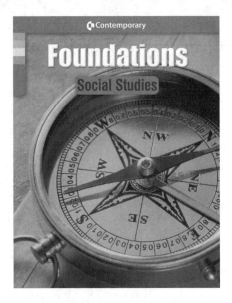

This book is divided into five units.

World History—the study of events that have shaped how people live and how they react to one another

U.S. History—the study of past events in the United States and the connections between these events

Civics and Government—the study of the responsibilities of citizens and the way governments work

Geography—the study of places around the world

Economics—the study of how people, businesses, and governments manage money

These special features in *Foundations: Social Studies* will help you learn the skills needed to understand social studies topics.

Writing Workshops—detailed instructions that will guide you through the four-step writing process: prewriting, drafting, revising, and editing

Background Information—details that will help you understand maps, charts, and cartoons

Language Tips—explanations, pronunciations, study hints, and background information that will help you understand what you are reading

Test Skills—a reminder that this skill is often tested on standardized tests

Posttest—a test, answer key, and evaluation chart so you will know how well you have mastered the skills

We hope you will enjoy *Foundations: Social Studies*. We wish you the best of luck with your studies!

Foundations

Contemporary's *Foundations* is a series of books designed to help you improve your skills. Each book provides skill instruction, offers interesting passages to study, and gives opportunities to practice what you are learning.

In addition to *Foundations: Social Studies*, we invite you to explore these books.

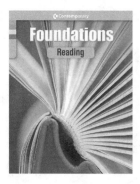

- In *Foundations: Reading*, you will read **practical information**, **nonfiction**, **poetry**, and **short stories**.
- You will learn to find the **main point** and the **details**; identify **fact, opinion**, and **bias**; make **inferences**; read **photographs** and **cartoons**; and understand **rhythm, rhyme, plot**, and **theme**.
- **Writing Workshops, Language Tips**, and **prereading questions** will help you become a better reader, writer, and thinker.

- In *Foundations: Writing*, you will practice the four steps to writing an essay: **prewriting, drafting, revising**, and **editing**.
- You will read and write five kinds of essays—**descriptive essays, personal narratives, how-to essays, essays of example**, and **comparison-and-contrast essays**.
- A language-skills workbook gives you **grammar, punctuation**, and **sentence structure** practice.
- **In Your Journal, With a Partner**, and **Language Tips** will help you become a better writer—and a better reader and thinker.

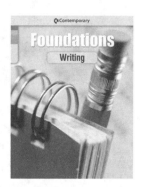

- In *Foundations: Math*, you will practice using **whole numbers, money, decimals, fractions, ratios**, and **percents**.
- Exercises will help you review the **addition, subtraction, multiplication**, and **division** facts; **round numbers**; **estimate** answers; and solve **word problems**.
- **Math Notes, On Your Calculator**, and **Language Tips** will help you improve your math skills.

- In *Foundations: Science*, you will learn about the **human body, plant biology, physics, chemistry**, and **Earth science**.
- You will practice putting events in **order**; reading **diagrams, charts**, and **graphs**; using the **scientific method**; and making **comparisons and contrasts**.
- **Try It Yourself!** activities will guide you through simple experiments so you will have a better understanding of what you have been reading about. **Writing Workshops** and **Language Tips** will help you use your reading and writing skills to think about science topics.

World History

WHAT IS HISTORY? It is a record of past events. The people who study the past are called historians. They study the people, conditions, and ideas that caused events to happen. Historians study events long after they happened. This distance of time helps them understand the effect the past has had on the present.

Chapter	What You Will Learn About	What You Will Read
1	Finding the Main Idea	WHO Working Around the World "Let Them Eat Cake" The End of Smallpox The Taj Mahal
2	Finding Details	An African Uprising The Collapse of the Soviet Union The Columbian Exchange The Life of a British Factory Worker
3	Summarizing	A Free, Democratic Poland Modernizing Russia *El Grito de Dolores!* Confucius and "Right Living"
4	Reading Photographs and Paintings	The Value of Freedom Governing in Africa: Zimbabwe Napoleon, the Hero Samurai Warriors
Review	World History	Economic Progress in Vietnam

After studying this unit, you should be able to

- find the main idea

- identify details

- summarize information

- read information in photographs and paintings

Chapter 1

Finding the Main Idea

Titles often signal what a chapter or a section of a book is about. That is, the title often tells the **topic** of a piece of writing. Chapter titles are clues to the topic of the whole chapter. For example, the author of a history textbook may write a chapter called "China in the Ninth Century." You can expect this chapter to be about China 1,200 years ago. One section in the chapter might be "Paper Money in China." When you read this section, you expect to find out how the Chinese used paper money.

Every piece of writing has a **main idea**. The main idea is the author's most important point about the topic. It is what the author wants the reader to think about. Chapters, sections, and paragraphs all have main ideas.

The title, or headline, of a newspaper article might be "Global Warming Harms Arctic Wildlife." The main idea of the whole article may be in the first paragraph: "Melting ice is changing the way animals live in the Arctic." You can expect each paragraph in the article to give examples of animals that are being affected by global warming.

WHO Working Around the World

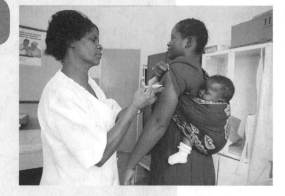

The World Health Organization (WHO) is "responsible for providing leadership on global health issues." This organization is part of the United Nations. It advises nations on good health policies so people in all countries will have healthier lives.

One of WHO's goals is to improve health care. WHO works with **developing nations**[1] to figure out how to provide health care for their people. Most people in these nations are poor and live far away from cities. WHO helps set up clinics and train doctors, nurses, and other health care workers in these nations.

As part of its goal to improve health care, WHO works to get drugs and **vaccines**[2] to poor nations. To do this, WHO asks drug companies in **developed nations**[3] to give drugs. For example, one U.S. drug company pledged $50 million worth of drugs to help fight river blindness in Africa.

---

[1]**developing nations**: countries working to build a higher standard of living and an economy based on industry

[2]**vaccines**: medicines given to people so they will not get certain diseases

[3]**developed nations**: countries that have a high standard of living and an economy based on industry

You may find it hard to believe that children still die from measles. Measles can be deadly in developing nations, however. WHO has helped get measles vaccines to African nations. This effort has resulted in many fewer deaths from measles in Africa.

Yellow fever is another deadly disease. In 2007, a group of West African nations worked with WHO to start a vaccination campaign. These nations planned to vaccinate 48 million people against yellow fever. Their goal was to end yellow fever in West Africa. With the help of WHO, millions of people will have healthier lives.

Look at how this passage is organized. It contains five paragraphs. The sentence that states the main idea of a paragraph is called the **topic sentence**. The other sentences in the paragraph describe or explain the main idea. Often the topic sentence is the first sentence in a paragraph. However, the topic sentence may be found anywhere in a paragraph.

◆ Write the sentence from the first paragraph that states the main idea of the passage.

_____

You are correct if you wrote the first sentence of the paragraph: **The World Health Organization (WHO) is "responsible for providing leadership on global health issues."**

◆ Underline the sentence that states the main idea in paragraph 4.

You should have underlined the **second sentence**.

◆ Now go back and underline the main-idea sentences in the other three paragraphs.

You should have underlined **the first sentence in paragraphs 2 and 3** and **the fourth sentence in paragraph 5.**

Strategy: How to Find the Main Idea

- Read the whole passage.
- Find the topic. *Whom* or *what* is the passage about?
- Find the main point that the author is making about the topic.
- Check that you have correctly identified the main idea. Ask yourself, "Do all the details support this idea?"

Exercise 1

Revolutions start for many reasons. What caused the French Revolution?

Read the passage. Then circle the best answer for each question.

LANGUAGE Tip

Notice the words *first*, *second*, and *third* in paragraph 1 of this essay. They help you understand how the essay is organized. Look for explanations of these three reasons in the paragraphs that follow.

"Let Them Eat Cake"

The French Revolution began in 1789 and ended in 1799. During this time, the **monarchy**[1] was overthrown. Nobles and **clergy**[2] lost their power. There were three main reasons for the revolution. First, the monarchy held absolute power. Second, the nobles and clergy had many **privileges**[3] that ordinary people did not. Third, France was facing serious economic problems.

French kings had complete power. France had a congress that was supposed to make laws. However, the French kings had not called it into session for 174 years. The king, not representatives of the people, made the laws. The king's power angered the people.

Marie Antoinette

The privileges of the nobles and clergy also led to problems. Nobles were the only people who could get high-level government jobs or become officers in the army. Nobles did not have to pay taxes. As a result, the cost of paying for the government fell on ordinary citizens. Three-quarters of all farmers rented land from the nobles and clergy. These farmers had little money left after they paid taxes and rent. They hated the privileges of the nobles and the rich clergy.

The middle class also hated the nobles and the clergy. The middle class was made up of merchants, lawyers, and doctors. These people worked hard to earn a living and pay taxes. However, they could not get top government or military positons.

The third reason for the revolution was France's economic problems. The government was not collecting enough money to pay its bills. The monarchy spent huge amounts of money on itself. The kings and queens had no idea how hard life was for their people. One story told about Queen Marie Antoinette shows how

---

[1]**monarchy:** government headed by a king, queen, or other nobles
[2]**clergy:** members of the priesthood
[3]**privileges:** advantages, benefits

little she cared about the people. The queen was told that the people could not afford bread. She is supposed to have said, "Let them eat cake."

Anger toward the monarchy came to a boil in 1789. Louis XVI finally had to call the congress into session. He was desperate for money. However, things quickly got out of hand, and the revolution began.

1. What is the passage about?
   (1) the French monarchy
   (2) the causes of the French Revolution
   (3) the privileges of the nobles and clergy
   (4) the economic problems of France

2. Which sentence states the main idea of the passage?
   (1) During this time, the monarchy was overthrown.
   (2) There were three main reasons for the revolution.
   (3) The nobles and clergy lost their power.
   (4) France was facing serious economic problems.

3. What is the topic sentence of paragraph 4?
   (1) The middle class also hated the nobles and clergy.
   (2) The middle class was made up of merchants, lawyers, and doctors.
   (3) They worked hard to earn their living and pay taxes.
   (4) However, they could not get top positions in government or in the army.

4. Which sentence best explains why the ordinary people hated the nobles and clergy?
   (1) Nobles and clergy collected rent from farmers.
   (2) Nobles and clergy did not pay taxes.
   (3) Nobles and clergy took the best jobs in government and the army.
   (4) Nobles and clergy had many privileges that they did not have.

5. Who had to pay taxes in France?
   (1) only farmers
   (2) only the middle class
   (3) farmers and the middle class
   (4) clergy who were landlords

Check your answers on page 187.

Exercise 2

Do you remember getting your measles vaccination? How about your mumps and chickenpox vaccinations? Vaccinations protect you from getting diseases. How were vaccines discovered?

Read the passage. Then circle the best answer for each question.

The End of Smallpox

We can thank Edward Jenner for stopping the spread of smallpox. In 1980, the World Health Organization (WHO) announced that smallpox had been wiped out. The disease was no longer a danger. People no longer needed smallpox vaccinations.

Dr. Edward Jenner

What did Edward Jenner have to do with getting rid of smallpox? Dr. Jenner lived in England in the 1700s. At that time, smallpox was a deadly disease. It killed thousands of people every year. It was especially dangerous for children.

Jenner worked in a farm area. People there said that milkmaids never got smallpox. Instead, they got cowpox from the cows they milked. This was a milder disease that spread among cows. Once a milkmaid had cowpox, she never seemed to get smallpox.

Jenner decided to investigate. He injected some of the cowpox virus into James Phipps, a healthy eight-year-old boy. He did not get smallpox. Jenner continued his experiment. He injected more children with cowpox. None of them got smallpox.

Jenner was convinced that injecting the cowpox virus into humans caused them to become immune to smallpox. They would not get smallpox after they were injected. He called what he injected a *vaccine*. Jenner wrote about his experiment in 1798.

At first, people did not believe him. Some people said that injecting a disease into a healthy person was immoral. However, within a few years, it was clear that the smallpox vaccine worked. People who were vaccinated against smallpox never got the disease.

Jenner's experiment has led to the discovery of other vaccines. Polio is another deadly disease. Polio patients can be crippled for life or even die. In the 1950s, Dr. Jonas Salk discovered the first polio vaccine. Vaccines have also been developed to fight mumps, measles, and chickenpox. These diseases have been nearly wiped out in the United States. Now WHO is working in poorer nations to end these diseases there too.

1. What is the topic of the passage?
   (1) smallpox
   (2) kinds of vaccines
   (3) the discovery of a vaccine against smallpox
   (4) Edward Jenner's life

2. Which sentence best states the main idea of the passage?
   (1) We can thank Edward Jenner for stopping the spread of smallpox.
   (2) In 1980, WHO announced that smallpox had been wiped out.
   (3) The disease was no longer a danger.
   (4) People no longer needed smallpox vaccinations.

3. From clues in paragraph 5, what does *immune* mean?
   (1) to be vaccinated
   (2) to give the disease to someone else
   (3) to become ill from a disease
   (4) to be protected against getting a disease

4. Which sentence states the main idea of paragraph 3?
   (1) Jenner worked in a farm area.
   (2) People there said that milkmaids never got smallpox.
   (3) Instead, they got cowpox from the cows they milked.
   (4) Once a milkmaid had cowpox, she never seemed to get smallpox.

5. Which sentence best states the main idea of paragraph 6?
   (1) Many people did not think that vaccinations would work.
   (2) Vaccinations protect people against disease.
   (3) People believed Jenner because of the success of the vaccinations.
   (4) Vaccinations were considered immoral.

6. Which sentence in paragraph 7 states the main idea of the paragraph?
   (1) Jenner's experiment has led to the discovery of other vaccines.
   (2) Polio is another deadly disease.
   (3) Vaccines have also been developed to fight mumps, measles, and chickenpox.
   (4) Now WHO is working in poorer nations to end these diseases there too.

Check your answers on page 187.

Exercise 3

People have many ways to honor the memory of loved ones. However, few have the money to build a tomb like the one built in India 350 years ago. How does your family honor those who have died?

Read the passage. Then circle the best answer for each question.

The Taj Mahal

The Taj Mahal is one of the most beautiful buildings in the world. It is also one of the saddest. Shah Jahan built it as a tomb for his wife Mumtaz Mahal.

Shah Jahan is perhaps the most famous Mogul ruler of India. *Mogul* is the name given to the emperors who ruled much of India from 1526 to 1857. The Moguls were Muslims who had invaded India from Afghanistan. Shah Jahan ruled from 1628 to 1658. This period is known as the Golden Age of the Mogul Empire.

The Taj Mahal

Shah Jahan first saw Mumtaz Mahal when she was 14. Their marriage, which took place when she was 20, was arranged. Shah Jahan loved Mumtaz Mahal and considered her the most beautiful woman in the world. During the next 19 years, they had 13 children. She often traveled with him around the empire. It was on such a trip that she gave birth to their 14th child. Mumtaz Mahal died shortly afterward.

In his grief, Shah Jahan hid himself in his palace. It is said that he cried for a week and that his hair turned gray. To ease his loss, he decided to build a beautiful tomb to honor the memory of Mumtaz Mahal.

The result was the Taj Mahal. Shah Jahan called it the "tower of light." It is made of white marble. Workers brought the marble 200 miles across the desert. The central part of the building is a square covered by a huge dome. Towers, called minarets, top each corner of the building. The walls are decorated with verses from the Quran, the holy book of Islam. Craft workers used turquoise, jade, sapphires, and other jewels to create patterns of flowers and shapes on the walls. A long narrow pool leads up to the front of the building. A white marble wall with tall columns surrounds the Taj Mahal. Inside and outside of the wall are gardens and walkways. It took 20,000 workers 20 years to build the Taj Mahal.

1. What is the topic of this passage?
    (1) burial places
    (2) the love between Shah Jahan and Mumtaz Mahal
    (3) beautiful buildings in India
    (4) Shah Jahan and the Taj Mahal

2. Which sentence states the main idea of paragraph 2?
    (1) Shah Jahan is perhaps the most famous Mogul ruler of India.
    (2) *Mogul* is the name given to emperors who ruled much of India from 1526 to 1857.
    (3) Shah Jahan ruled from 1628 to 1658.
    (4) This period is known as the Golden Age of the Mogul Empire.

3. What is the main idea of paragraph 3?
    (1) Shah Jahan and Mumtaz Mahal had an arranged marriage.
    (2) Mumtaz Mahal died after the birth of their 14th child.
    (3) Shah Jahan and Mumtaz Mahal had a happy marriage.
    (4) Mumtaz Mahal went everywhere that Shah Jahan went.

Check your answers on page 187.

Writing Workshop

Prewriting

In this chapter, you read about Dr. Edward Jenner. Make a list of people you know or that you have read about who have helped others. Choose one person to write about.

Drafting

Write a sentence that states your main idea. This sentence should name the person you are writing about and tell what the person did. Then add sentences that explain your main idea. Every sentence you add should help readers understand the main idea.

Revising

Be sure that your main idea is clearly stated and supported by your other sentences.

Editing

Capitalize a person's title only when it is used as part of the person's name.

> Dr. Jenner created a smallpox vaccine. The doctor helped end smallpox.

Chapter 2

Finding Details

As news reporters gather information, they ask *Who? What? Where? When? Why?* and *How?* The answers to these questions make up the details of their news stories. **Details** are facts, examples, and reasons. Details give information about the main idea.

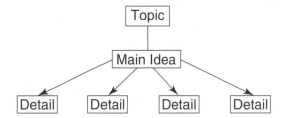

How can you use these questions to improve your reading skills in social studies? Look for the answers to the questions *Who? What? Where? When? Why?* and *How?* as you read a passage. The answers will help you understand the author's main idea.

An African Uprising

In the 1880s, Great Britain, France, Italy, Germany, Belgium, Portugal, and Spain each turned parts of Africa into European colonies. The African people and their resources were used to increase the wealth of the European nations that controlled the colonies.

German East Africa is one example of such a colony. Looking at its history shows how some European countries treated their colonies. It also shows how Africans fought back. The nations that are today Tanzania, Rwanda, Burundi, and part of Mozambique made up German East Africa.

German East African troops

From the beginning, German officials expected the colony to send its wealth to Germany. Africans had to pay taxes. They were forced to work on roads and other building projects. Africans could not practice their religions. They were forced to grow cotton instead of food because German factories needed cotton to make cloth.

In 1905, Kinjikitile Ngwale led an uprising against the Germans. He gave his followers "magic water." He said it would protect them against German bullets. His supporters attacked German forts with spears and arrows. However, the magic water did not work. German machine guns killed row after row of African fighters. The Germans then went through the colony, destroying villages, crops, and animals.

The uprising lasted until 1907. Several hundred Germans died. Between 75,000 and 200,000 Africans, including women and children, died. Many died from hunger.

◆ **Write the letter of the correct answer for each question.**

_____ 1. Who led the uprising in German East Africa?

_____ 2. Why did the Africans rebel against their German rulers?

_____ 3. Where was the uprising?

_____ 4. When did the uprising occur?

_____ 5. How did the Germans respond to the uprising?

_____ 6. Why did the Africans think they were safe from German guns?

(a) They destroyed villages, crops, and animals.

(b) They thought magic water would protect them from bullets.

(c) paying taxes, doing forced labor, not being able to practice their religions, and being forced to grow cotton

(d) Kinjikitile Ngwale

(e) 1905–1907

(f) German East Africa

Here are the answers: **1.** (d), **2.** (c), **3.** (f), **4.** (e), **5.** (a), **6.** (b).

Did you notice that the questions are asking *Who? What? Where? When? How?* and *Why?* All the details explain the main idea of the passage. As you read, try to picture in your mind the details that the author is describing. Imagine soldiers burning the fields, for example.

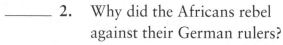

Strategy: How to Find Details

- Ask the questions *Who? What? Where? When? Why?* and *How?*
- Picture in your mind what the passage is explaining.
- Think about how the details fill in or support the main idea.

Exercise 1

LANGUAGE Tip

Older maps use the name *USSR* for the Soviet Union. These initials stand for the "Union of Soviet Socialist Republics."

For more than 70 years, the government of the Soviet Union controlled millions of people. Why did it fall apart in 1991? How had it failed its people?

Read the passage. Then answer the questions.

The Collapse of the Soviet Union

In 1917, Communists overthrew the Russian ruler and took control of the government. By 1922, the old Russian Empire had become the Soviet Union. It included Russia, 19 other republics, and several smaller regions in Europe and Asia.

The Communists kept tight control over the government and the economy. Only members of the Communist Party could run for public office. Only Communists could hold government jobs. People could not criticize the government. They could not practice their religions freely. All factories and

Russians had more goods in their stores after the end of communism.

land were owned by the government. Government officials made all decisions about what was produced and how much was produced. They also decided the price of all goods. Many of the nation's resources were used to pay for tanks, planes, and missiles.

Poor economic planning and high military costs led to many problems. Grocery store shelves were often empty. In winter, there were fuel shortages. People lacked many things that Americans took for granted such as cars, stoves, refrigerators, and televisions. Housing was in short supply. Whole families, including grandparents, lived together in two-room apartments.

In 1985, Mikhail Gorbachev became head of the Soviet Union. He understood the frustration and anger of the people. He tried to reform the government and the economy. Factory managers were given freedom to decide what to produce and how much to produce. He encouraged people to start their own businesses. Farmers could sell food themselves instead of selling only to government stores.

The reforms did not work at first. More shortages occurred. Prices rose. Workers lost their jobs when factories closed because of poor management. The people began to demonstrate against the government. In 1991, Gorbachev resigned. By the end of the year, the Soviet Union had collapsed. The republics declared their independence. They decided the future would be better if they were on their own.

1. Where was the Soviet Union?_____

2. How did the Communists control the government of the Soviet Union?

_____

3. What problems were the result of poor economic planning and the high cost of the military?

_____

_____

4. Who first tried to reform the government and the economy in the Soviet Union?

_____

5. Why did he try to reform the Soviet government?

_____

6. When did the Soviet Union collapse?_____

Check your answers on page 187.

Exercise 2

Do you like tomatoes? How about onions? Did you know that onions most likely came from Asia, but tomatoes came from North America?

Read the passage. Then circle the best answer for each question.

The Columbian Exchange

Christopher Columbus arrived in the Americas in 1492. At that time, millions of people were already living here. They lived in a variety of environments. Some lived in hot deserts. Others lived in forests where the climate was mild. People also lived in the mountains and along the seacoasts. Different kinds of plants grew in each of these environments. The Europeans who came to the Americas had never seen many of these plants. Since many of the plants could be eaten, Europeans began to eat new foods.

Two of the foods that were new to Europeans were potatoes and corn. In time, potatoes and corn became important food crops in Europe. Soon, Europeans were carrying these foods along trade routes that stretched to China. Tomatoes, peanuts, squash, pumpkins, peppers, and pineapples were also carried east on the trade routes—and so were turkeys. Both Europeans and Asians began to grow many of the beans that had come from the Americas—lima beans, navy beans, and kidney beans.

Foods were also carried from Europe to the Americas. Europeans brought grapevines and wheat to the Americas. They brought sugarcane, which had originally come to Europe from Asia. Before long, sugarcane became the major crop on the Caribbean islands. Other crops carried from Europe were apples, bananas, pears, peaches, lettuce, and onions. In the 1500s, the Spanish brought horses to the Americas. Chickens, cattle, and pigs were also carried from Europe.

This trading of foods and animals is known as the Columbian Exchange. Unfortunately, the Europeans brought more than foods and animals. They also brought diseases such as smallpox and measles. Native Americans had no resistance to these new diseases. As a result, as many as 90 percent of Native Americans living in Spanish colonies died.

1. Who started the trade of food between Europe and the Americas?
   (1) the Spanish
   (2) people on the Caribbean islands
   (3) Christopher Columbus
   (4) Asians

2. What was the Columbian Exchange?
   (1) the death of many people from new diseases
   (2) the movement of foods and animals between Europe and the Americas
   (3) the new trade routes to Asia
   (4) trade between Colombia and the rest of the world

3. When did the Columbian Exchange take place?
   (1) in the late 1400s and early 1500s
   (2) in the 1600s, when settlers arrived in America
   (3) in the 1700s, when the United States became independent
   (4) in the 1900s, when people made frequent trips on airplanes

4. Where did sugarcane first come from?
   (1) Asia
   (2) the Caribbean islands
   (3) Europe
   (4) the Americas

5. How did potatoes and corn get to Asia?
   (1) Native Americans took them there.
   (2) Asians began traveling to the Americas.
   (3) They had been grown in Asia for many years.
   (4) Europeans took them there from the Americas.

6. Why did so many Native Americans die in Spanish colonies?
   (1) They were worked too hard.
   (2) They died when they moved to new environments.
   (3) They had no resistance to European diseases.
   (4) They got sick from food brought from Europe.

Check your answers on pages 187–188.

Exercise 3

Do you know someone who works in a factory? What is working in a factory like today? How different is it from what is described in this passage?

Read the passage and complete the exercise.

LANGUAGE Tip

Suffix

The suffix *-ize* means "to cause to be." Here are some *-ize* words:

industrialize   criticize

modernize   memorize

The Life of a British Factory Worker

The first nation to **industrialize**[1] was Great Britain. It was the first for several reasons. It had deep rivers where boats could travel, and it had good harbors. Both were important for moving **raw materials**[2] and goods from one place to another. Great Britain also had large supplies of iron and coal. Iron was used to build machines, ships, and railroads, and coal powered the steam engines that ran them. Most of all, Great Britain had people. The population of Great Britain increased from 5 million in 1700 to 9 million in 1800.

The growing population supplied workers for the new factories. Factory work was not easy. Most workers had come from farms. They were used to doing a wide variety of tasks and working outdoors.

Factory work was much different. Workers did the same job every day. It was often dangerous work. The machines had no safety features. A worker who was not careful could lose fingers or even a hand. Workers worked 6 days a week, 12 to 16 hours a day. It was hard for them to stay alert because they were so tired. They did not dare stop working. They were afraid that their wages would be cut or that they would be fired. They had breaks only when the foreman said they could. Lunch and dinner breaks were often only 30 minutes. Wages were just a few dollars a week.

Most early factory workers were women. They were paid about half what men were paid. Children were paid even less. Even some 6-year-old children worked in factories. Children, too, worked 16-hour days, 6 days a week. If they did not work as hard as the foreman thought they should, they were beaten.

---

[1]**industrialize:** change from the use of hand tools to machines

[2]**raw materials:** materials that are used in factories to make products

1. Where did the first industrialization take place?_____

2. How were factory and farm work different?_____

   _____

3. When did Great Britain's population reach 9 million people? _____

4. Who were the workers in the early factories? _____

5. What prevented workers from stopping work? _____

6. Why were factory workers always tired? _____

Check your answers on page 188.

Writing Workshop

Prewriting
Make a list of problems that people have today. Choose one problem to write about.

Drafting
Write a sentence that states your main idea. Then write sentences that answer the questions *Who? What? Where? When? How?* and *Why?*

Revising
Read each sentence to be sure all the details are clear. Improve any unclear sentences.

Editing
Check that every sentence begins with a capital letter and ends with a period, question mark, or exclamation point.

Chapter 3

Summarizing

How do you decide which TV shows to watch? You may look at the newspaper to find summaries of the programs. A **summary** briefly tells you the most important details about a program.

The following descriptions summarize three TV programs. The summaries give a general idea of what the programs are about.

Mary Ann Walker	Architects discuss the building of Egypt's pyramids.
Saturday News Special	Peter Kent compares the week's news with events in history.
America at War	Veterans of World War II are interviewed.

Read this passage. As you read, look for the main idea and the most important details. Think about how you would summarize the passage.

A Free, Democratic Poland

When World War II ended in 1945, Josef Stalin was the leader of the Soviet Union. He wanted to make sure that Poland had a Communist government. Poland was located on the southern border of the Soviet Union. Stalin wanted Poland to be a barrier between Russia and Western Europe.

In 1945, a temporary government was put into place in Poland. It was controlled by Communist leaders. In 1947, the Communist Party won the election and set up a new government. However, the election was not fair. It had been fixed so only members of the Communist Party could win.

The Poles did not accept their Communist masters without a fight. In 1956, the people rioted against the government. A reform party came to power. It made some changes during the 1960s and early 1970s. However, the Soviet Union still held power over Poland. The Polish government was still controlled by Communists.

In 1980, Polish workers started a series of strikes because of their working conditions and low wages. Lech Walesa saw a chance to make changes. He was a

Solidarity march

shipyard worker in the city of Gdansk. Walesa started a labor movement called Solidarity. The organization soon spread to other Polish cities. Solidarity members across Poland began protesting their poor economic conditions. As a result, the government jailed Walesa and other labor leaders in 1981. Solidarity was outlawed.

When the Polish people protested, the government freed Walesa and the others. However, the protests against the government continued. By 1989, Solidarity broke the Communists' hold on the nation. Free elections were held, and Lech Walesa became president of Poland in 1990.

Now read the following summary of "A Free, Democratic Poland."

Poland's government was controlled by Communists from 1945 until 1990, when Lech Walesa, leader of the Solidarity movement, was elected president.

In the summary, many of the details in the original paragraph are left out. A summary states only the main idea and the most important details. The writer does not use exact wording from the passage. Instead the writer restates the information in his or her own words.

◆ **Summarizing helps you remember important ideas. Reread the paragraph above about summarizing. Then answer this question in your own words.**

How is a summary different from the original passage?

You may have answered: **A summary includes the main idea and the important information, and it is written in your own words.**

Strategy: How to Summarize Information

- Read the whole passage carefully.
- Find the topic, the main idea, and the most important details.
- Explain the information in your own words.
- Check to see that your explanation matches the information in the original passage.

Exercise 1

Modernizing means "making things modern, or up-to-date." For example, using a computer modernizes how messages are sent. What are some other examples of doing things in a modern way?

Read the passage. Then complete the exercise.

Modernizing Russia

Peter the Great became tsar, or ruler, of Russia in 1672. At the time, Russia was considered backward compared with nations such as France and England in Western Europe. During Peter's 35 years in power, he tried to change Russia into a modern nation.

Peter set up a system of primary schools. He started schools to train Russians in mathematics, science, and technology. Some Russians were sent to Europe so that they would have a Western education.

Peter also focused on creating Russian industry. He brought in Western technology to start new mining, cloth-making, and iron-manufacturing businesses. Transportation systems were also improved. To help with these reforms, Peter hired people from Western Europe to train Russians.

Peter the Great

In addition, Peter tried to make social reforms. His greatest success had to do with the appearance of Russians. Peter ruled that all Russians except for serfs (farm workers) and priests had to wear Western-style clothes. Peter also decided to get rid of beards. At one time, beards had been popular in all of Europe. By the 1700s, however, they were no longer the style in Western Europe. Peter ruled that nobles had to shave their beards. Priests and serfs were allowed to keep their beards.

Any noble who refused to shave his beard had to beware of meeting Peter. It is said that if Peter came upon a noble with a beard, he would take a razor to the beard. He is said to have actually yanked some beards out by their roots. Peter was 6 feet 9 inches tall and weighed close to 300 pounds. He might well have been able to do this!

1. What is the topic of the passage?
   (1) the growth of Russian industry
   (2) modernizing Russian education
   (3) how Peter the Great modernized Russia
   (4) changes in the appearance of Russians

2. Which sentence best summarizes the information in paragraph 4?
   (1) Serfs and priests did not have to cut their beards or wear Western-style clothing.
   (2) Peter wanted to modernize the clothing and appearance of Russians.
   (3) Peter ruled that beards had to be shaved off.
   (4) Nobles had to wear Western-style clothing.

3. What does *backward* (in paragraph 1) mean?
   (1) focusing on the wrong things
   (2) not up-to-date
   (3) facing the wrong way
   (4) not being in front

4. Check ✔ all the reforms mentioned in this passage.
   _____ (a) New iron-manufacturing businesses were started.
   _____ (b) Nobles were forced to serve in the military or government.
   _____ (c) Canals were built to speed transportation.
   _____ (d) Schools were started to train Russians in math and science.
   _____ (e) Some Russians were educated in Western Europe.

5. Which sentence summarizes the passage?
   (1) Peter the Great wanted Russians to look more like Western Europeans.
   (2) Russia became a modern country during Peter the Great's rule.
   (3) Changes ordered by rulers are never popular.
   (4) Peter the Great reformed schools, industry, and dress in Russia.

Check your answers on page 188.

Exercise 2

People in many parts of the world are fighting for freedom and democracy. What do you think makes people willing to fight for freedom?

Read the passage. Then circle the best answer for each question.

El Grito de Dolores!

"The Cry of Dolores!" is the name given to Mexico's first fight for independence. This fight for independence began in the church of Dolores on September 16, 1810. *Dolores* means "sorrows."

On that day, Father Miguel Hidalgo rang his church bell to gather the people. He made an emotional speech to them. He asked them to join him in the fight for freedom from Spain. He said to them, "My children, will you be free?"

A statue of Father Hidalgo

Father Hidalgo was a creole. Creoles are people born in the Americas to Spanish parents. The people that Hidalgo was speaking to were Native Americans and mestizos. (Mestizos are part Native American and part Spanish.) Creoles belonged to a higher social and economic class than Native Americans and mestizos. They had wealth, but they did not have political power. They were tired of being ruled by Spain.

The government sent soldiers to fight against Hidalgo's forces. Less than a year after his speech, Hidalgo was captured and killed. However, it was not the end of the independence movement. Father José Morelos, another creole, took charge of the uprising. He and his army fought government forces until 1815. Like Hidalgo, Morelos was also captured and killed.

Independence finally came in an unusual way. In 1821, General Augustin de Iturbide formed an **alliance** with creole, mestizo, and Native American leaders. Iturbide, who was a creole, was a general in the Spanish army in Mexico. The general and his followers overthrew the Spanish government. Then Iturbide named himself Emperor Augustin I. After more than 300 years, Mexico was free of Spain. However, this independence did not bring the freedom for mestizos and Native Americans that Father Hidalgo had hoped for. Life did not improve for them.

---

alliance: partnership; agreement to work together

1. What is the topic of the passage?
   (1) how Mexico gained its independence from Spain
   (2) Father Hidalgo's part in helping Mexicans gain independence
   (3) the role of creoles in gaining Mexican independence
   (4) General Iturbide's role in gaining Mexican independence

2. Which sentence most accurately summarizes why creoles wanted independence?
   (1) Creoles hated the Spanish.
   (2) Creoles would have more power if Spanish rule ended.
   (3) Creoles wanted to help poorer Mexicans by overthrowing Spanish rule.
   (4) Creoles thought they would be richer if they overthrew the Spanish.

3. Which sentence best summarizes the information in paragraph 4?
   (1) Father Morelos continued the fight for independence after Father Hidalgo was killed.
   (2) Father Morelos failed the same way that Father Hidalgo had failed.
   (3) Independence from Mexico was worth dying for.
   (4) Even after Father Hidalgo died, the fight for independence continued.

4. Which fact is *not* included in paragraph 5?
   (1) The alliance included General Iturbide, mestizo and Native American leaders, and other creoles.
   (2) When independence was declared, General Iturbide named himself emperor.
   (3) Father Hidalgo's speech began the fight for Mexican independence.
   (4) Spain had ruled Mexico for more than 300 years.

5. Which point is *not* important enough to be stated in a summary of the passage?
   (1) *Dolores* means "sorrows."
   (2) An army of mestizos and Native Americans joined Hidalgo to fight for independence.
   (3) Both Father Hidalgo and Father Morelos were killed by government forces.
   (4) General Iturbide was able to unite local leaders to overthrow the government.

Check your answers on page 188.

Exercise 3

Confucius believed that each person in society has a duty to live by a code of good conduct. What is your personal code of good conduct?

Read the passage. Then answer the questions.

Confucius and "Right Living"

Confucius was a philosopher and teacher who lived in China from 551 to 479 BCE. His students called him Kong Fuzi. Confucius lived during a time of many wars and great social change. To help people deal with these problems, he developed a new philosophy. His philosophy, or system of ideas, is called Confucianism.

Confucius wanted China to become a stable and just society. He believed his philosophy could help China reach that goal. Confucianism praised loyalty, respect for elders, and hard work. It included a code of conduct called "right living."

Confucius's system was based on five sets of relationships. These relationships established a person's place in society. The relationships were

- between a ruler and those who were ruled
- between parent and child
- between husband and wife
- between older brother and younger brother
- between friend and friend

*KONG-FÚ-TSÉ or CONFUCIUS
the most Celebrated Philosopher of China.*

Confusius

The last relationship was between equals. But in the first four relationships, the second person was always inferior, or less important. For example, the ruler was clearly superior, or more important, than any of the people he ruled. Parents were superior to their children. This was true even if the child was 50 years old.

Each person had duties and responsibilities to the other person in the relationship. Even a ruler had duties and responsibilities to those he ruled. The less important person owed respect, loyalty, and obedience to the superior person. The superior person had a duty to take care of the less important person. Confucius believed that if people lived by this code, society would once again be peaceful and just.

1. Confucius described five sets of relationships. Write a summary describing the relationships.

   _____

   _____

2. Write a summary of the information in the last paragraph about duties and responsibilities.

   _____

   _____

Check your answers on page 188.

Writing Workshop

Prewriting
Confucius developed a code of conduct for developing a peaceful and just society. Do you agree with his ideas about duties and responsibilities? State your opinion. Then make a list of reasons for your opinion. Choose one reason to write about.

Drafting
Write a main-idea sentence stating why you agree or disagree with Confucius's ideas. Then add sentences that explain your main idea in more detail. Each sentence in your paragraph should explain or support the main idea.

Revising
Writers often state their main idea in the first sentence so readers will understand what they are reading about. Sometimes they restate the main idea (using different words) in the last sentence. Write a final sentence for your paragraph that restates the main idea.

Editing
Look for run-on sentences. Fix them by writing two shorter sentences or by adding connecting words such as *and* or *but*.

Chapter 4

Reading Photographs and Paintings

LANGUAGE Tip

On October 3, 1990, East Germany and West Germany were united. Today the country is called "Germany." Its official name is the Federal Republic of Germany.

News articles often have photographs. Most textbooks have photos or pictures of paintings. These images are more than decoration. They provide information.

To get the most from a photo or a painting, it is important to "read" the image. When you read an image, you analyze it. You study the details and carefully read the caption.

Look at this photograph. Then read the passage.

The Value of Freedom

In 1945, at the end of World War II, Germany was divided into four zones. Great Britain, France, the United States, and the Soviet Union each took control of one zone. The city of Berlin, the capital of Germany, was also split into four sections.

By 1949, Great Britain, the United States, and France had joined their zones together. They created the Federal Republic of Germany, or West Germany. The three nations also joined their sections of Berlin. It became known as West Berlin. The Soviets created the German Democratic Republic, or East Germany. The Soviet section of Berlin was called East Berlin.

An East German border guard leaps over barbed wire dividing East and West Berlin.

The people of West Germany quickly recovered from World War II. They had jobs, food, and freedom. But in East Germany, unemployment was high. There were shortages of goods, and Communists kept a tight hold on the government. However, if East Germans were unhappy, they could walk across the border to a better life.

In August 1961, the East German government decided to stop people from crossing the border. A barbed wire fence was put up so East Berliners could no longer go into West Berlin. Later a concrete wall was built. Armed border guards patrolled the wall. The wall was up for 28 years. During that time, about 5,000 East Germans climbed over it or tunneled under it. It is estimated that 125 people were killed trying to escape East Berlin.

Examine the photo in detail. You see a man leaping over barbed wire. But this is not just any man. The caption says that the man is an East German border guard. People are standing behind the guard. They seem to be watching what he is doing.

What expressions do you see on the faces of the people behind the guard? They do not seem to be either angry or excited. One man is standing with his hands in his pockets. Maybe the people don't yet understand what is happening.

Who is this man? Where is he? Why is he jumping over barbed wire? The caption and the passage help you understand the photo. In turn, the photo helps you understand the passage.

Every photo or painting expresses the point of view, or opinion, of the maker. The photographer who took this photo had an opinion about the border guard.

◆ **Why do you think the photographer took this picture of the border guard?**

_____

_____

Here are some possible answers:

   The photographer admired the courage of the guard.

   The photographer wanted to show that people were risking their lives because they knew freedom was valuable.

Strategy: How to Read Photographs and Paintings

- Look at the details in the image.
- Read the caption and any writing that is in the photo or painting.
- Think about the photographer's or artist's point of view.
- Use the image to visualize the information you are reading about.

Exercise 1

Candidates for public office depend on volunteers to help them win. Have you ever volunteered to help a candidate?

Read the passage. Then answer the questions.

LANGUAGE Tip

Use this pronunciation guide as you read the passage.

Zimbabwe	zim BAH bway
Rhodesia	roh DEE zhah
Mugabe	moo GAH bee

Governing in Africa: Zimbabwe

In the 1880s, European nations divided up Africa into colonies. They controlled the colonies until the mid-20th century. Beginning in the 1950s, black Africans demanded their independence. By 1980, most of the colonies were independent nations. Most of these new governments were run by black Africans.

However, whites in several colonies refused to let this happen. In Southern Rhodesia, for example, whites forced a new constitution through the parliament. It made sure that whites would keep control of the government. Then, the white government declared Southern

This voter is cheering at a rally for candidates of the ZANU-PF Party. The next day, voters elected a majority of ZANU-PF candidates.

Rhodesia's independence from Great Britain. However, neither Great Britain nor the United Nations accepted this declaration. They thought the new government's policies toward its black citizens were unfair.

One person opposed to the new government was Robert Mugabe. He became head of the ZANU Party in the late 1970s. ZANU stands for "Zimbabwe African National Union." Finally in December 1979, Great Britain and the colony's political parties came to an agreement. The country became independent. The new nation was named Zimbabwe.

Mugabe was elected leader, or prime minister, of the new government. In 1987, his party joined with another party to become the ZANU-PF Party. By 2000, Mugabe and ZANU-PF had controlled Zimbabwean politics for 20 years. During that time, the government passed laws that allowed land to be taken from white farmers and given to black Africans. Mugabe's party also changed the way representatives were elected to parliament. The old law named districts by race. The new law allowed all districts to elect black or white representatives.

Today Zimbabwe faces many serious problems. The policy of taking land from white farmers caused many of these farmers to leave the country. The loss of these farmers and the lack of rain for several years led to food shortages. Prices for all goods began to rise very fast. The country owed large debts to international banks that it could not repay. In 2005, Zimbabwe had an unemployment rate of 80%, and more than 60% of the population was living in poverty. These problems, along with government corruption, have hurt the popularity of Mugabe and the ZANU-PF party.

1. What are the people in the photo doing?

   _____

2. Notice that many people in the photo are wearing T-shirts that have a picture of a man on them. Who do you think that man is?

   _____

3. Do these look like rich people, middle-class people, or poor people?

   _____

4. Why do you think the photographer took this picture?

   _____

5. From the information in the passage, how do you think the people of Zimbabwe feel about the ZANU-PF party today?

   _____

   _____

Check your answers on page 188.

Exercise 2

A painting can help you understand what you are reading about. Is the man on horseback in this painting leading soldiers, or is he running away from something?

Read the passage. Then complete the exercise.

Napoleon, the Hero

Napoleon Bonaparte graduated from the French military academy in 1785. Then he joined the army as a lieutenant. When the French Revolution began a few years later, he sided with those who were against the monarchy.

Napoleon was a military commander by 1793. He led his troops against France's fiercest enemy, Great Britain, and won an important battle. Two years later, he stopped an uprising against the new French government. In 1797, Napoleon's army defeated the Austrian and Italian armies. As a result of these victories, the defeated nations had to give up land to France. By then, Napoleon was a national hero.

This portrait of Napoleon was painted in 1801.
He was at the peak of his power.

Napoleon Bonaparte seized power in France in 1799. He declared himself emperor five years later. It was not difficult for Napoleon to take control. France had not had a stable government since 1789. Napoleon ruled France for much of the next 15 years.

For most of the time that Napoleon led the country, France was at war with Great Britain and other European nations. France gained more and more territory. However, events started turning against France in 1812. By 1814, Napoleon was forced into exile. He was ordered to live outside of France. However, Napoleon escaped in 1815. He came back to France and ruled the country again—but only for 100 days. Then the great general was defeated at the battle of Waterloo. Napoleon was sent into exile on an island in the Atlantic Ocean. He died there in 1821.

1. What is the topic of this passage?

   _____

2. What detail in the painting tells you that the man is Napoleon Bonaparte?

   _____

3. Which description best tells how Napoleon looks in this painting?
   (1) angry and unhappy
   (2) in command of what is happening
   (3) not sure of which way to go
   (4) frightened because he cannot control his horse

4. What do you think Napoleon is doing in this painting?
   (1) hurrying to get out of a storm
   (2) trying to turn his horse around
   (3) leading the way for others to follow
   (4) going out for a ride

Check your answers on page 188.

Since ancient times, nations have defended themselves. Do you know anyone who is a soldier or who has served in the military?

Read the passage. Then circle the best answer for each question.

Samurai Warriors

The figures in this painting may look strange to you. However, what they are doing probably does not look odd. These men are samurai. They are fighting with swords.

Samurai belonged to Japan's military class. This social class developed about one thousand years ago. Nobles hired samurai to defend them and their property. The right to be a samurai was passed down from father to son. Future samurai were trained from early childhood. When a young man was ready to take on the duties of a samurai, he was given two swords. These swords were his for life. They marked him as a samurai.

Over time, a code of conduct developed for how a samurai should act. The code was called Bushido. The word *Bushido* means "warrior's way." A samurai was supposed to be brave in battle and loyal to his lord. He was trained to endure hardship. If a samurai did something to disgrace himself or his lord, it was his duty to kill himself. This was also the action expected of a samurai who was defeated in battle.

The samurai warriors defended Japanese lords. They were important to Japanese society from 1100 to the late 1800s.

1. What is the topic of this passage?
   (1) the class system in Japan
   (2) the development and training of the samurai class
   (3) the life of a samurai
   (4) Bushido

2. What does the man on the right have that marks him as a samurai?
   (1) shoes
   (2) two swords
   (3) uniform
   (4) chest protector

3. If the samurai who is on the ground has been defeated, what is he supposed to do?
   (1) Go to his lord to be punished.
   (2) Beg the winner for mercy.
   (3) Give his swords to the winner.
   (4) Kill himself.

4. From looking at the painting, what do you think is the artist's opinion of samurai?
   (1) Samurai are fierce fighters.
   (2) Samurai are well-trained.
   (3) Samurai sometimes lack courage.
   (4) Samurai are muscular.

Check your answers on pages 188–189.

Writing Workshop

Prewriting

In this chapter, you learned how photos and paintings can help you visualize what you are reading about. Make a list of several photos or paintings in this book that you think are interesting. Choose one to describe.

Drafting

Write a main-idea sentence describing what is happening in the photo. Then add sentences that describe the details in the picture. Each sentence should help your readers understand what is happening.

Revising

With a partner, look at each detail in the picture. Try to add descriptive words that will help your readers see, feel, hear, smell, or taste what you are describing.

Editing

Check that you have used present tense verbs to describe details in the picture. Present tense verbs are words such as *is, are, fight, march, builds, are wearing,* and *is making*.

Review – World History

What do you know about the Vietnam War? Do you know anyone who served in the war in Vietnam?

Read the passage. Then circle the best answer for each question.

Economic Progress in Vietnam

Life in Vietnam was disrupted by war from 1945 until 1975. The Communists of North Vietnam finally took control of South Vietnam in 1975. They united the two parts of the country into one nation. Communists controlled the government and the economy of the new nation of Vietnam.

The new nation was very poor. The government controlled all land and all industry. It created an economic program to improve the standard of living. Businesses were told what to produce, how much to produce, and what to charge for goods. Small farms were combined into large farms. Farmers became workers on these state-run farms.

Life did not improve under the Communists. Roads and bridges had been destroyed during the long war years. There was no money for repairs. There was no money to build power plants or set up irrigation systems.

By the early 1990s, it was clear that government policies were not working. Changes were made in 1992. The government decided to invite foreign companies to invest money by building factories. Vietnamese citizens were encouraged to start private businesses.

Modern Vietnam

By the early 21st century, Vietnam had an unemployment rate of only 2.4 percent. It had sold more than $32 billion worth of goods to other nations. These goods included rice, coffee, tea, and clothing. Vietnam had been able to buy more than $36 billion worth of products such as machinery, cotton, grain, cement, and motorbikes from other countries. Its major trading partners were Japan, the United States, Australia, Singapore, South Korea, and China.

1. What is the main idea of paragraph 2?
   (1) Life did not improve under the Communists.
   (2) Vietnam was very poor after the war.
   (3) The Communists tried to improve conditions in Vietnam.
   (4) Communists took industries and land from the people.

2. Which detail in the photograph is the best example of the growing wealth of the Vietnamese?
   (1) the buildings
   (2) the number of motorbikes on the street
   (3) the face mask being used because of pollution
   (4) the fancy clothes

3. According to paragraph 5, which of the following is an important import in Vietnam?
   (1) coffee
   (2) rice
   (3) cement
   (4) clothing

4. Which sentence best summarizes paragraph 1?
   (1) After many years of war, the people of Vietnam were happy to have a new government.
   (2) The new nation of Vietnam was controlled by Communists.
   (3) The new nation had many problems because farms were very small.
   (4) Vietnam was created by joining the North and the South under a Communist government.

5. According to the passage, which statement about Vietnam is most accurate?
   (1) Machinery and tea are imported into Vietnam.
   (2) The United States does not trade with Vietnam.
   (3) One problem facing the new nation was the lack of roads and bridges.
   (4) Unemployment is very high.

Check your answers on page 189.

U.S. History

EACH NATION of the world has a history that is shaped mostly by the people and the events within its borders. However, people and events beyond a nation's borders can also shape its history. Wars and trade are two examples of this.

History tells us about the past. However, history also offers clues to a nation's present and future. By studying past mistakes, historians can tell us what went wrong. They can also help us see when we were at our best as a nation.

Chapter	What You Will Learn About	What You Will Read
5	Sequence	From Typewriters to Text Messaging Pioneers of Flight Settling Early California The Montgomery Bus Boycott
6	Cause and Effect	The Dust Bowl The Rise of Labor Unions The Wild West How the Car Changed America
7	Problem and Solution	Civil Disobedience Earth Day The Trail of Tears President Roosevelt Tackles a Problem
8	Comparison and Contrast	A Father's Changing Role Rosie the Riveter and Condoleezza Rice A Lesson from Lincoln's Life Washington and DuBois
Review	U.S. History	Japanese Internment in World War II

After reading this unit, you should understand

- sequence
- cause and effect
- problem and solution
- comparison and contrast

Chapter 5

Sequence

Sports announcers tell their listeners exactly what is going on in a game. Here is a play-by-play account of a baseball game.

> **The pitcher leans forward and waits for the sign from the catcher. Here is the windup and the pitch. The batter swings. It is a high fly ball. The leftfielder catches it easily. One out!**

Sports announcers describe each action in **sequence**, or time order. They tell what happens first, what happens next, and so on. As a result, you can easily follow the events of the game. You can even imagine the events in your mind.

Knowing the order in which events occurred will help you understand history. Many historical accounts—like the play-by-play account of the baseball game—report a series of actions or events in the order they happened. History tells a story of events that are linked together in a sequence.

Watching for dates is one good way to keep track of sequence. Clue words such as *first, second, third, last,* and *after* can also help you figure out time order. As you read the following passage, underline the dates and the word clues that signal time order.

From Typewriters to Text Messaging

Chances are you have a cell phone. It is small enough to fit in your pocket because it is powered by a tiny microprocessor. This tiny chip is the computer in your phone. It is powerful enough to let you communicate around the world. Would you believe that the first computer was so big that it needed a room the size of a ballroom? The computer was the ENIAC. It was introduced in 1946.

Computers small enough for ordinary use were not sold until the 1960s. These computers came in pieces that buyers had to put together. Most early computers were bought by businesses. However, some were bought by people who used computers as a hobby. Two men turned their hobby into a business. They founded Apple Computer. In 1976, the company launched the Apple I. The following year, it released the Apple II. That same year, Commodore International released the Commodore PET. Also in 1977, the Tandy Company released the TRS-80. This was the beginning of desktop computing, but all the machines were still big and heavy.

As people began to use computers at work, they saw how quickly the computers helped them perform tasks such as typing. Soon people wanted computers at home.

Desktop computers got smaller and cheaper. In 1981, the first portable computers were sold. They were smaller—about the size of portable sewing machines. Over time, portable computers became the thinner, lightweight laptops that we now use. Today computers can weigh as little as two pounds. However, they are more powerful than any computer that most people would have imagined in the 1980s.

Did you underline four dates? How many clue words for time order did you find? The time-order clue words are *first, following year, same year, soon, first, over time,* and *today.*

◆ **Use information in the passage to fill in the missing events in the time line.**

1946		1976 1977	1981
ENIAC is introduced.	_____	_____	_____

Compare your time line with the one below.

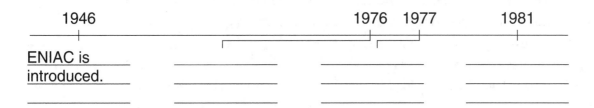

1946		1976 1977	1981
ENIAC is introduced.	Apple I is launched.	Apple II, Commodore PET, and Tandy TRS-80 are released.	The first portable computers are sold.

Strategy: How to Understand Sequence

- Find the topic. What event or time period is described?
- Look for dates and clue words such as *next, before, later, after,* and *finally* that will help you understand the sequence.
- If possible, create a time line to summarize the events.
- Check to see how the events are related to one another.

Since ancient times, people have dreamed of flying. What famous Americans made this dream come true? Who are the heroes in the history of flight?

Read the passage and answer the questions.

Pioneers of Flight

These newspaper headlines announced important events in the history of flight.

Flying Machine Soars Three Miles in Teeth of High Wind
Millions Roar Welcome to Lindbergh
Amelia Earhart Flies Across Ocean

On December 17, 1903, a crowd gathered on a windy beach near Kitty Hawk, North Carolina. Orville Wright watched as his brother, Wilbur, steered the flying machine they had designed. Wilbur soared like a bird in the amazing invention. This first plane was powered by a gas engine. "It's a success!" Orville said after Wilbur flew the first mile. Then Wilbur glided in the air for two more miles before he finally landed the plane.

On May 20, 1927, Charles Lindbergh climbed into the cockpit of his plane, the *Spirit of St. Louis.* He took off from New York and arrived in Paris 33½ hours later. Lindbergh was the first man to make a nonstop solo flight across the Atlantic Ocean. One newspaper called this "the greatest feat of a **solitary**[1] man in the records of the human race." Fans flocked to parades. They welcomed home their new American hero—"Lucky Lindy."

Exactly five years later, another pilot made history. Her name was Amelia Earhart. On the night of May 20, 1932, she took off from Newfoundland in a single-engine red plane. After a very dangerous flight, she landed in Ireland 15 hours later. Earhart was the first woman to fly across the Atlantic Ocean alone. She said, "I hope that the flight meant something to women in **aviation.**[2] If it has, I shall feel it was **justified.**"[3] Amelia Earhart soon became known as "Lady Lindy, First Lady of the Air."

---

[1]**solitary:** alone
[2]**aviation:** related to airplanes
[3]**justified:** shown to be reasonable

Charles Lindbergh

Amelia Earhart

1. Use the information in the passage to fill in the events on the time line.

December 17, 1903	**May 20, 1927**	**May 20, 1932**
_____ _____ _____	_____ _____ _____	_____ _____ _____

2. Why do you think Amelia Earhart was nicknamed "Lady Lindy"?

_____

3. Why was the Wright brothers' three-mile flight so important?

_____

Check your answers on page 189.

Exercise 2

Spain did not begin to settle California until the 1700s. Why did Spain finally decide to settle California? What kinds of settlements did it build?

Read the passage and complete the exercise.

Settling Early California

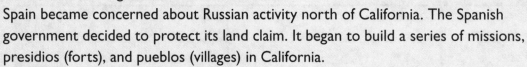

Juan Rodriguez Cabrillo visited the coast of California in 1542. He was the first Spanish explorer to see California. He was looking for gold. Cabrillo claimed the area for Spain. Spain wanted more colonies like the colonies it had in Mexico and Peru. These colonies were rich in gold and silver. However, Cabrillo did not find gold in California. Because there was no gold there, the Spanish were not interested in settling California.

Two hundred years later, Spain changed its mind about settling California. In the 1760s, Spain became concerned about Russian activity north of California. The Spanish government decided to protect its land claim. It began to build a series of missions, presidios (forts), and pueblos (villages) in California.

The priests who ran the missions were trying to convert Native Americans to the beliefs of the Roman Catholic Church. Each mission had a house for the priest and a church. It also had living quarters and workshops for Native Americans, orchards, and barns. The presidios protected the missions and villages. The presidios themselves were small villages. Settlers lived in the forts with the soldiers. The forts had storehouses, workshops, and stables.

The building of the first mission and fort in California began on July 16, 1769. This was San Diego. It was located on the coast of Southern California. A year later, the Mission San Carlos de Monterey was built north of San Diego. The next year, Mission San Luis Obispo was built a little farther north. The plan was to separate missions by distances that could be walked in one or two days. A traveler would be able to find a safe place to stay by going from mission to mission. Missions were also close enough that one fort could protect several missions. Eighteen missions had been built along the California coast by 1800. The final three missions were built by 1817.

At the same time, the Spanish built four presidios and four pueblos. After building the presidio at San Diego, the Spanish built forts at Monterey in 1770, San Francisco in 1776, and Santa Barbara in 1780. The first pueblo was founded in 1777 at San José. Los Angeles was founded four years later. Other pueblos grew up around the presidios.

Add the date for each of these events.

1. _____ Los Angeles is founded.

2. _____ The presidio at Monterey is built.

3. _____ The mission and fort at San Diego are built.

4. _____ The last mission is built.

5. _____ Mission San Luis Obispo is built.

Use your answers to questions 1–5 to fill in the dates on this time line. Then write a very brief summary of each event on the lines below the date.

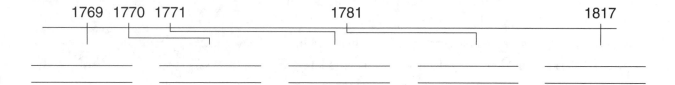

1769 1770 1771   1781   1817

Answer these questions in the space provided.

7. Why did Spain decide to settle California?

_____

8. What buildings were found at a mission?

_____

Check your answers on page 189.

Exercise 3

In the 1950s, the public bus system of Montgomery, Alabama, was racially segregated. Bus drivers could order African Americans to give up their seats to white people. Would you have given up your seat?

LANGUAGE Tip

During the 1950s and 1960s, many people worked to bring equal rights to African Americans. This effort is known as the Civil Rights Movement.

Read the passage and complete the exercise.

The Montgomery Bus Boycott

Rosa Parks

On Thursday, December 1, 1955, Rosa Parks boarded a bus in Montgomery, Alabama. She sat down in the first row of the middle section of seats. This area was open to blacks if all whites were seated. However, at the next stop, some whites got on. They filled all the "white-only" seats. One white man was left standing.

Then the bus driver, James Blake, said, "Y'all better make it light on yourself and let me have those seats." Three black people rose, but Rosa Parks did not move.

"When he saw me still sitting," Parks recalled, "he asked if I was going to stand up and I said, 'No, I'm not.'" Blake replied, "Well, if you don't stand up, I'm going to have to call the police and have you arrested." Parks said, "You may do that." Moments later, a police car took Parks to the county jail. She was charged with breaking the law.

News of her arrest spread quickly. E. D. Nixon, a former head of the National Association for the Advancement of Colored People (NAACP), called the Reverend Ralph Abernathy on Friday morning, December 2. They arranged a meeting with other black ministers and leaders for Friday evening. At the meeting, most agreed to boycott, or not use, the buses for one day.

On Monday morning, December 5, a torn piece of cardboard appeared at the main downtown bus stop. It said, "PEOPLE DON'T RIDE THE BUSES TODAY. DON'T RIDE FOR FREEDOM." The one-day boycott was a success.

Ministers and community leaders met again that afternoon and chose a new leader—Dr. Martin Luther King Jr. He gave a speech at a community meeting that same night. He said, "One of the great glories of democracy is the right to protest for right." The people were moved by his words, and they decided to continue the boycott.

Nearly a year later—on November 13, 1956—the Supreme Court outlawed bus segregation. On December 21, the bus company was forced to follow the Supreme Court's ruling. After a long boycott, blacks once again rode Montgomery's buses.

Number the events in correct time order.

_____ E. D. Nixon calls the Reverend Ralph Abernathy.

_____ Rosa Parks is arrested.

_____ A sign is posted at the bus stop announcing a boycott.

_____ The Supreme Court outlaws bus segregation.

_____ Rosa Parks refuses to give up her seat to a white man.

_____ Martin Luther King Jr. becomes the leader of the protest.

Check your answers on page 189.

Writing Workshop

Prewriting

In this chapter, you read about some major events in American history. What are the major events that make up your personal history? Make a list of events in your life and the dates they occurred. Your list might include a special birthday, your first job, your wedding, or the birth of a child.

Review your list. Next, choose five of the most significant events. Then create a time line showing these events.

Drafting

Write a paragraph describing one of the events in your time line. Add details so your readers understand what happened and why the event is important to you. Use time order to organize the information in your paragraph.

Revising

Check that the details are logically organized. Add time-order words such as *first, then, later,* and *on the next day.* They help your reader understand the sequence of events.

Editing

Check your verbs to be sure you have used the past tense correctly. Past tense verbs tell about events that have already happened. Examples:

I worked at the new hardware store.

I was working when I fell off the ladder.

I had worked only six weeks when **I ended** up in the hospital.

Chapter 6

Cause and Effect

Picture the details described in this weather report.

> **A blizzard struck the area today. High winds and heavy snowfall have made traveling dangerous. Many airports have canceled flights. Several schools have been closed.**

The details in the weather report are arranged to show cause and effect. The **cause** is the reason something happens. The **effect** is the result. In the weather report, the cause is the blizzard. The effects are airports being shut down and schools being closed.

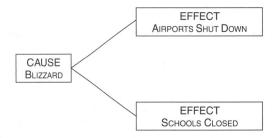

Analyze the cause-and-effect relationships in these two statements.

- Because of the storm, the power went out. (The words *because of* signal a cause.)
- The streets were icy, so cars were skidding. (The word *so* signals an effect.)

Weather can influence day-to-day events. It has also influenced American history. As you read the passage, think about how each event caused another event to occur.

The Dust Bowl

The Dust Bowl was a farming disaster that took place in the Plains states during the 1930s. From North Dakota to Texas, wind blew the topsoil away from 50 million acres of land. This area became known as the "Dust Bowl."

The problems began in early 1930. Too many cattle were grazing on the land. Because farmers had new, larger plows, they were able to plant larger and larger areas. People did not know how to take care of the land.

A severe drought caused the land to dry out. Topsoil began to blow away, causing terrible dust storms. Big clouds of dust made the sky look black. The crops dried up. Thousands of families were forced to give up their land and leave their homes.

Most families headed for California, hoping to find jobs. These people were called "Okies," although they did not all come from Oklahoma. John Steinbeck's famous book *The Grapes of Wrath* is about the Okies who went west.

A farmer and his sons walk in a dust storm in Oklahoma in 1936.

Look at how the passage is organized. The writer arranges the details in time order to explain the sequence of events. He also analyzes the causes and effects.

◆ **Can you identify which events are causes and which are effects? Next to each statement below, write *cause* or *effect*.**

_____ Farmers had new, larger plows.

_____ Windstorms blew away the dry soil.

_____ Farms were turned into deserts.

_____ Farm families left their farms and went west.

The first two statements explain causes. They answer the questions "Why did the Dust Bowl occur?" and "Why did the topsoil blow away?"

The last two statements explain effects. They answer the question "What were the results of the Dust Bowl?"

Strategy: How to Understand Cause and Effect

- Pay close attention to the sequence of events.
- Notice whether one event caused another event to occur.
- Look for clue words such as *because, as a result, so,* and *therefore*.
- Check the topic sentence to see if it states a cause-and-effect relationship.

Why do people join labor unions? Do you think labor unions protect workers?

Read the passage and answer the questions.

The Rise of Labor Unions

As the number of factories increased in the United States during the late 1800s, working conditions grew worse. Most of the factory workers then were immigrants who came from Europe. In 1905, the average man worked 10 hours a day, 6 days a week. Average pay was about 25 cents an hour. The situation was even worse for women and blacks. By 1906, more than 60% of American workers were unable to earn enough money to support a family.

Factory work was usually boring, and the conditions were often dangerous. Many people worked in sweatshops. A sweatshop is a factory where people work long hours. Sometimes the workers even live in dormitories at the factory. Sweatshops in the early 1900s were usually dirty, unsafe, and overcrowded.

Many children also worked in the factories and sweatshops. In the early 1900s, almost two million children were factory workers. In the South, about one-third of all the workers in cotton mills were children. Many families were unable to send their children to school.

Workers were unhappy with the working conditions, so labor unions began to grow. Unions fought to solve the workers' problems. They wanted the factory owners to increase wages and decrease the number of hours people had to work. They also fought to end child labor. The owners did not want workers to join unions. As a result, conflicts arose between the workers and the factory owners. In the United States, workers were not granted the right to join unions until the 1930s.

PART A

1. What angered the factory workers?
   (1) too many European immigrants
   (2) terrible working conditions
   (3) police involved in labor conflicts
   (4) American cities

2. What is the topic sentence in the last paragraph?
   (1) Workers were unhappy with working conditions, so labor unions began to grow.
   (2) Unions fought to solve the workers' problems.
   (3) Conflicts arose between the workers and the factory owners.
   (4) Workers were not granted the right to join unions until the 1930s.

3. According to the passage, what happened when labor unions demanded better working conditions?
   (1) Employers fired workers and used machines.
   (2) Employers started treating workers fairly.
   (3) Workers became happy, healthy employees.
   (4) Conflicts often broke out between factory owners and workers.

PART B

1. How much did an average man earn each week in the early 1900s?

   _____

2. List three conditions that made sweatshops bad in the early 1900s.

   (a) _____

   (b) _____

   (c) _____

Check your answers on page 189.

Exercise 2

The Wild West is a period of American history dating from 1865 to 1900. Why do you think there were so many outlaws during the Wild West period?

Read the passage and complete the exercise.

The Wild West

John Wesley Hardin was a preacher's son with a bad temper. "They tell a lot of lies about me. They say I killed six or seven men for snoring, but it isn't true. I only killed one man for snoring." This famous outlaw from Texas admitted killing 44 people.

The terror of Jesse James and his gang remains a legend in U.S. history. Bank holdups, train robberies, and killings were the way the gang did its business. Butch Cassidy and his Wild Bunch earned their fame as train robbers. Posters offered rewards for killers, outlaws, and crooks. These criminals were products of the Wild West. Why was the West so wild?

After the Civil War ended in 1865, many Southerners were bitter. Some held grudges against the North. John Wesley Hardin said he was not running away from justice. He was running away from **injustice**.[1] Hardin continued to be angry about the injustices people suffered in the South after the Civil War. Jesse James never lost the taste for violence and killing that had been part of his life while he served as a **Confederate**[2] soldier.

Jesse James

During the 1880s, terrible weather and a depression in the cattle country meant disaster for cowboys. As a result, many cowboys were out of work. Some, like the Wild Bunch, turned to a life of crime.

The lack of law officers and jails also made the West wild. Many men cared more about staying alive than wearing a sheriff's badge. Some people carried out their own justice. They held "necktie parties," where they hanged the outlaws they caught.

---

[1]**injustice:** unfairness
[2]**Confederate:** one who fought for the South in the Civil War

PART A

Write *cause* or *effect* on the lines.

1. _____ Because they had lost the Civil War,

   _____ many Southerners felt bitter toward the North.

2. _____ Jesse James had fought in the Civil War;

   _____ therefore, he knew about violence and killing.

3. _____ Many cowboys were out of work

   _____ as a result of terrible weather and a depression in 1880s.

4. _____ Since there were not enough law officers and jails in the Wild West,

   _____ some citizens hanged outlaws at "necktie parties."

5. _____ John Wesley Hardin killed a man

   _____ because the man had been snoring.

PART B

Circle the best answer for each question.

1. What is the main idea of the passage?
   - (1) Terrible weather meant disaster for cowboys.
   - (2) The Wild Bunch earned its fame by robbing trains.
   - (3) The West was wild because men turned to crime and there were not enough law officers.
   - (4) "Necktie parties" were one way people tried to keep order.

2. According to the passage, why was Jesse James so violent?
   - (1) He liked holding up banks and robbing trains.
   - (2) A depression in the cattle country made him angry.
   - (3) He had had an unhappy childhood.
   - (4) He got a taste for killing when he was a soldier.

Check your answers on page 189.

Exercise 3

How has the automobile influenced American life?

Read the passage and complete the exercise.

How the Car Changed America

During the 1920s, American society began to feel the effects of the car. New factories and suburbs sprang up in areas that were once wilderness. Main streets became dotted with traffic signals. Gas stations and hot dog stands opened. By the end of the 1920s, motels and billboards were scattered along the highways.

More roads connected the city and the country, so farmers began driving regularly into cities and towns. City people rode miles into the country for picnics. The romance of the road encourgaged millions to take long car trips. Many followed the popular slogan "See America First." They drove from Florida to California to see tourist spots.

The growth of the car industry had bad effects too. The number of car accidents increased. Traffic jams, street noise, and smoke often caused major problems. Some parents blamed cars for encouraging teenagers to have sex. Criminals used "getaway" cars to escape the police.

Will Rogers said this about Henry Ford: "It will take a hundred years to tell whether you have helped us or hurt us, but you certainly didn't leave us like you found us."

PART A

1. The topic of the passage is
   - (1) the growth of the car industry
   - (2) teenage behavior in the 1920s
   - (3) the effects of cars during the 1920s
   - (4) the causes of car accidents and traffic jams

2. Farmers began driving more often into cities because
   - (1) they had friends in the new suburbs
   - (2) they had more roads to use
   - (3) they liked visiting gas stations and hot dog stands
   - (4) they wanted to see tourist spots

3. Which statement describes a negative (bad) effect of the car?
   (1) Main streets became dotted with traffic signals.
   (2) People drove long distances to see America.
   (3) Factories were built in the countryside.
   (4) Criminals used cars to escape from the police.

PART B

List two good effects and two bad effects of cars in the 1920s.

Good Effects: (1) _____ (2) _____

Bad Effects: (1) _____ (2) _____

Check your answers on page 190.

Writing Workshop

Prewriting

In this chapter, you read how the car affected American society in the 1920s. Write a list of machines or inventions that have a positive (good) effect on your life. Choose one machine from your list to write about.

Drafting

Write a topic sentence in the form of a question: What would happen if _____ had never been invented? Then write a paragraph to answer your question.

Revising

Help your reader by adding cause-and-effect clue words to your paragraph. Words that signal causes are *because*, *due to*, and *since*. Words that signal effects are *so*, *therefore*, *for that reason*, and *so that*.

Editing

Be sure you have used complete sentences. Look at the examples.

   Incomplete: Because I do not like spending time in the kitchen.
   Complete: Because I do not like spending time in the kitchen, I got a microwave.
   Incomplete: Since he has caller ID.
   Complete: William knows when I'm calling him since he has caller ID.

Chapter 7

Problem and Solution

Every day, people write letters to advice columnists in newspapers about their personal problems. The beginning of each letter usually describes the situation that is causing the problem. The writer wants answers to questions such as these:

- What should I do?
- What are my choices?
- How can I change or improve my life?

In response, the advice columnist offers a solution. An article that describes a problem and then offers a solution follows a **problem-and-solution** pattern.

The details in many social studies passages are arranged in a problem-and-solution pattern. Read the following passage to find out how one U.S. citizen from the 1800s reacted to a problem. Then answer the questions about the passage.

Civil Disobedience

In 1846, the United States declared war on Mexico. Henry David Thoreau was against the war. He believed that the goal of the war was to increase slave territory in the United States. "Unjust laws exist," he wrote, "but shall we obey them?"

Thoreau believed that the answer was to "resist" the U.S. government. He said the government was "the *slave's* government also." To protest the war, Thoreau refused to pay his **poll tax** to Massachusetts. As a result, he was thrown into jail. Thoreau said that a prison was the only house in a slave state where a free man could live with honor.

Henry David Thoreau

Thoreau's essay "Civil Disobedience" offered solutions for the problem of injustice. He believed that people had the right to rebel against laws they thought were wrong. Thoreau favored nonviolent protest. His ideas later inspired Martin Luther King Jr. King believed in Thoreau's solutions. He organized marches and other nonviolent protests as a way of speaking out against laws that permitted racial injustice.

poll tax: a fee people had to pay before they could vote

◆ **Answer the questions in the space provided.**

What problem did Thoreau discuss in his essay "Civil Disobedience"?

_____

_____

According to Thoreau, what right did people have to solve this problem?

_____

_____

Thoreau's essay discussed the problem of **injustice**. Thoreau felt that people had **the right to rebel against laws that they believed were wrong.**

Causes and effects are often included in social studies passages that discuss a problem and a solution. An event may cause a problem. For example, the war against Mexico caused a problem for Thoreau. The problem caused him to face the question of slavery.

Solutions to problems can have lasting effects. One hundred years later, Thoreau's essay "Civil Disobedience" affected how Martin Luther King Jr. protested unjust laws in the United States.

Strategy: How to Understand Problem and Solution

- Identify the problem facing a person, a group, or a nation.
- Find the solution. What action was taken to improve the situation?
- Look for causes and effects. Why did the problem arise? What were the results of the solution?
- Think about whether the solution was successful.

Exercise 1

Why was the goal of the first Earth Day? Why do you think that Earth Day has been held every year since 1970?

Read the passage. Then answer the questions.

LANGUAGE *Tip*

Suffix

The suffix *-ist* means "someone who specializes in." An **environmentalist** is a person who works to improve the environment. Here are some other *-ist* words:

chemist	dentist
artist	typist

Earth Day

We often hear information about global warming, greenhouse gases, and pollution. These are not new problems. The United States has been an industrial nation for more than 150 years. In the nation's beginning, most Americans were farmers. By the mid-1800s, however, more and more factories were being built. The factories burned coal and pumped pollution into the air. In addition, they dumped their **wastes**[1] into streams and rivers. Growing cities also polluted the air and water.

By the mid-1900s, the United States was facing serious danger to the **environment.**[2] **Smog**[3] hung over many cities, making people ill. In 1953, smog shut down schools and businesses in Los Angeles for most of October. The year before, about 200 people had died from the smog over New York City. Rivers were becoming more polluted with chemicals and sewage. There was so much waste in the Cuyahoga River in Cleveland, Ohio, that the river caught fire in 1969.

---

[1]**wastes:** useless material left from manufacturing; garbage, trash, ashes
[2]**environment:** everything around us, including plants, rivers, and weather conditions
[3]**smog:** polluted air

Growing numbers of Americans became concerned about the damage to the environment. Congress had passed some laws in the 1950s to protect against air and water pollution. However, environmentalists did not think the laws were tough enough. They realized that the nation needed to understand that damage was being done. People needed to work together to save planet Earth.

That message came on April 22, 1970, the first Earth Day. Gaylord Nelson, a U.S. senator from Wisconsin, was a leader in organizing Earth Day. He estimated that 20 million Americans spent the day learning about the environment and demonstrating for reforms. Their actions encouraged Congress and the president to do something about the problem. During the next 10 years, 13 important laws were passed to protect our air, land, and water.

Today Earth Day is celebrated all around the world. Environmentalists use Earth Day to teach about the environment. They demonstrate for reforms that will protect Earth. They also encourage people to plant trees, pick up litter, and improve parks.

1. What problem did Senator Nelson hope to highlight on Earth Day?
   (1) reasons people were giving up farming
   (2) the number of people dying from smog
   (3) the Cuyahoga River fire
   (4) damage to the environment

2. How did the first Earth Day show Congress that Americans wanted to solve this problem?
   (1) Americans wrote letters to Congress.
   (2) Businesses stopped polluting the air.
   (3) Millions of Americans took part in Earth Day activities.
   (4) Earth Day has been celebrated every year since 1970.

3. What effect did Earth Day have on Congress?
   (1) Congress passed a law to ban smog.
   (2) The president gave a speech to Congress on Earth Day.
   (3) Congress passed 13 laws to protect the environment.
   (4) Many members of Congress took part in Earth Day.

Check your answers on page 190.

Exercise 2

How would you feel if you were forced to move out of your home and your neighborhood? Why was a Native American tribe forced to leave its home?

Read the passage and answer the questions.

The Trail of Tears

In the early 1800s, cotton was "king" in the South. Some Native American tribes lived in the southeastern United States. Many were living on land that could be used for growing cotton. Georgia was the cotton-growing state where most Cherokee lived. Georgia pressured the U.S. government to force the Cherokee to leave.

Because of pressure from Georgia, Congress took action. It passed the Indian Removal Act in 1830. According to this law, Native Americans had to give up their land. In exchange, they could settle in new territories west of the Mississippi River. President Andrew Jackson thought this was a fair solution to a tough problem. He said, "This unhappy race are now placed in a situation where we may well hope that they will share in the blessings of civilization. . . ."

To the Cherokee in Georgia, the Indian Removal Act was not a blessing. Instead, it was a curse. The Cherokee did not agree to move. They refused to leave their homeland. In 1838, President Van Buren enforced the Indian Removal Act. Federal troops rounded up

The Trail of Tears by Robert Lindneux

more than 17,000 Cherokee in Georgia. They marched the Cherokee toward their new land in the territory now known as Oklahoma.

John G. Burnett, an army private, described the journey: "I saw the helpless Cherokees arrested and dragged from their homes. . . . I saw them loaded like cattle or sheep into 645 wagons and headed for the West. . . . The trail of the **exiles** was a trail of death." About 4,000 Cherokee died along the way. This forced march became known as the "Trail of Tears."

Ralph Waldo Emerson, a well-known writer, was shocked by this cruel event in U.S. history. He wrote, "Such a denial of justice, and such deafness to screams for mercy were never heard . . . since the earth was made."

exiles: people driven from their homes

1. Before the Civil War, what was the most valuable crop in the South?_____

2. Why did Georgia want the Cherokee to leave the state?

   _____

3. What was the Indian Removal Act?

   _____

4. What was President Jackson's opinion of the Indian Removal Act?

   _____

5. How did the Cherokee respond to the Indian Removal Act?

   _____

6. What was the "Trail of Tears"?

   _____

Check your answers on page 190.

Exercise 3

What would you do if banks were not safe places to keep money? How do people react when they lose faith in the government?

Read the passage and complete the exercise.

LANGUAGE Tip

Franklin D. Roosevelt is the only person who has served more than eight years as president of the United States. The 22nd Amendment, passed in 1951, limits a president to two four-year terms in office.

President Roosevelt Tackles a Problem

The Great Depression of the 1930s brought unemployment and suffering. The economy plunged and feelings of panic and fear soared. Americans lost faith in their government. Franklin Roosevelt became president in 1933. He hoped to raise people's spirits and to boost the economy. In his first **inaugural address**, he made a statement that has become famous: "The only thing we have to fear is fear itself."

Franklin D. Roosevelt delivering his first radio address

Out of fear, people were rushing to their banks to withdraw their money. The first crisis facing Roosevelt was the banking problem. Two days after his inauguration, Roosevelt declared a "bank holiday." The government closed all the banks in the country for four days. Congress then passed the Emergency Banking Act. The act gave the government the power to inspect banking methods and records. To reopen, banks had to meet the government's standards.

Next, Roosevelt held his first "fireside chat." He spoke to Americans about the banking problem over the radio. "My friends, . . . I want to tell you what has been done in the last few days, why it was done, and what the next steps are going to be." He asked everyone to trust the banking system. "It is safer to keep your money in a reopened bank than it is under the mattress." Roosevelt's radio talk calmed people's fears. Many people hurried to banks to deposit their savings.

Roosevelt's regular radio talks made people feel better. Americans felt that they were working with Roosevelt to solve the problems of the Great Depression. Roosevelt himself said that his solutions might not always work. He practiced this approach to problem solving: "Take a method and try it. If it fails, admit it frankly and try another."

inaugural address: speech a president (or other public official) makes when sworn into office

Circle _T_ for true or _F_ for False.

T　F　**1.**　The Great Depression caused suffering, panic, and fear.

T　F　**2.**　The first problem Roosevelt solved was unemployment.

T　F　**3.**　During the "bank holiday," people rushed to the banks to withdraw their savings.

T　F　**4.**　Congress passed the Emergency Banking Act to help solve the banking problem.

T　F　**5.**　During his first fireside chat, Roosevelt explained his actions, the reasons for his actions, and his future plans.

T　F　**6.**　When the banks reopened, people hid their money under their mattresses.

T　F　**7.**　Roosevelt was sure that his solutions to problems would always be successful.

Check your answers on page 190.

Writing Workshop

Prewriting
In this chapter, you read about President Roosevelt's fireside chats. Because of these talks, people felt they could trust him. While he was president, many Americans wrote him letters. Make a list of problems you think the current president should try to solve.

Drafting
Write a letter to the president about one problem from your list. Give background information about the problem. End your letter by suggesting solutions.

Revising
Have you included enough details so the president can understand how this problem has affected you? Have you provided clear examples?

Editing
Be sure you are using the pronouns _I_ and _me_ correctly. _I_ is used as a subject, and _me_ is used as an object. Examples:

    I want better health care for all Americans.

    My friends have told **me** they feel the same way.

Chapter 8

Comparison and Contrast

> Take a test drive in the Cruiser.
> Check out the comfort and performance.
> Look at the price. Then shop around.
> You will see—the Cruiser beats all other SUVs.

This ad asks you to think about how the Cruiser and other SUVs are alike and how they are different. When you think about how things are alike, you are **comparing** them. When you think about how things are different, you are **contrasting** them. This approach is called **comparison and contrast**.

Many social studies passages show comparisons and contrasts. They tell how people, situations, or ideas are similar and different. Sometimes writers use a comparison-and-contrast pattern to point out changes that have occurred over time.

Learn what family life was like before and after the Civil War. Read the following passage. Underline the clue words that show comparisons and contrasts.

A Father's Changing Role

Before the **Civil War** (1860–1865), most fathers worked near their families on farms and in small towns. Even city workers had jobs close to their homes. Family life was usually centered around the father and the home.

However, in the late 1800s, cities grew. This changed family life. The father's role changed. Working-class men began to ride streetcars to work. They took jobs farther away from their homes. They spent more and more time away from their families.

Civil War: the war between the U.S. federal government and 11 southern states that wanted to separate from the Union

Before the Civil War, the father's world was still tied to his family. After the war, the worlds within the family grew apart. The shop, office, and factory were for men. In contrast, the home and school were for women and children.

The father's absence from home sometimes caused problems for children. In the past, fathers and sons had been close. Now some sons felt lost without their fathers. Young men found that adjusting to work and adulthood was more difficult.

Did you underline the clue words *however* and *in contrast*? These words signal differences. The growth of cities after the Civil War made the father's role different.

The passage shows two contrasting pictures of the father. First, imagine a father spending most of his time with his family. Then, imagine a father spending most of his time at his job.

◆ **Where did men, women, and children spend most of their time *after* the Civil War? Fill in the chart.**

Family Members	Where Was Time Spent?
men	
women and children	

Men began to spend most of the time in the **shop, office, or factory**. Women and children spent their time at **home and at school**.

Strategy: How to Understand Comparison and Contrast

- Find the topic. What people, ideas, or situations are compared or contrasted?

- Search for details that explain the topic. What is alike? What is different?

- Look for clue words that signal comparisons and contrasts. Examples include *like*, *similarly, in contrast, instead,* and *however.*

Exercise 1

What was the role of women during World War II? How is that different from the role that women have today?

Read the passage. Then complete the chart.

Rosie the Riveter and Condoleezza Rice

She rolled up her shirtsleeves and wore overalls. She carried a lunch bucket. She punched a time clock in a factory. She built war planes, navy ships, and army tanks. A national hero was born. Her name was "Rosie the Riveter."

Rosie appeared on posters and magazine covers. She called on American women to serve their country during **World War II**.[1] Women took the challenge. They worked in defense plants across the country. Meanwhile, millions of men fought overseas.

Rosie was not a real woman. She was a symbol of all the women who worked hard during the war. She represented **patriotism**.[2] However, after the war, people forgot about Rosie the Riveter. Men coming home from the war took over her job.

During the 1950s and 1960s, a woman's place was in the home. But some women continued to work outside the home. Then more women began going to college. By the 1970s and 1980s, many women were becoming doctors, lawyers, and professors. Women were also becoming world leaders.

Today Rosie the Riveter has been replaced with other role models. Condoleezza Rice is one of these role models. In 2005, Rice became the first African American woman to serve as **secretary of state**.[3] Unlike Rosie, Rice wore business suits. Rather than working in a factory for an eight-hour shift, she traveled around the world in a private jet. Instead of welding and riveting, she met with presidents and prime ministers. They held talks about nuclear arms, terrorism, and human rights. Condoleezza Rice is not a symbol. She is a real person. Her name frequently appears on lists of the most powerful women in the world.

These two contrasting images show how the role of women has changed. During wartime, Rosie the Riveter worked for freedom. Today Condoleezza Rice has a similar goal. However, how she works is very different from how Rosie worked.

---

[1]**World War II:** the 1939–1945 conflict between the Axis Powers (Germany, Italy, and Japan) and the Allies (France, Great Britain, the United States, the Soviet Union, and China)

[2]**patriotism:** loyalty to one's country

[3]**secretary of state:** the member of the president's cabinet who is responsible for relationships between the United States and other countries

Rosie the Riveter

Condoleezza Rice

	Rosie the Riveter	Condoleezza Rice
1. date		
2. work clothes		
3. place of work		
4. job		
5. purpose of work		

Check your answers on page 190.

Exercise 2

What makes a political leader popular? Would President Lincoln win an election if he were alive today?

Read the passage and complete the exercise.

A Lesson from Lincoln's Life

What was in the pockets of **Abraham Lincoln**[1] on the night he died? He had a pair of glasses, some money, and a pocket knife. The knife may have dated back to the time when he had lived in a small Illinois town. These items are stored at the **Library of Congress**.[2]

There was also a news story in his pocket. The article had been written during the last year of the Civil War. It gave Lincoln a little praise for the job he was doing. Lincoln had not received much public praise.

Unlike most modern presidents, Lincoln often met with everyday Americans. As president, he was under great pressure. Yet he talked to mothers whose sons were missing because of the war. He gave advice to wives whose husbands were in prison.

These meetings were demanding. For strength, Lincoln read the Bible each night. The Bible reminded him that true wisdom "comes from God and not from man."

Lincoln might not be accepted as a leader today. He was not a handsome man. He talked about moral strength coming from God. He tried not to criticize those who opposed him. In contrast, today's political **candidates**[3] seem to place more importance on style than on **moral values**.[4] They know that presenting a smooth image on TV wins votes. They spend a lot of time and money criticizing their opponents.

Today's leaders could learn a lesson from Lincoln. As president, he defended his beliefs. He paid little attention to the praise or criticism of others. Lincoln found that his strength came from his faith and his moral values.

---

[1]**Abraham Lincoln:** 16th president of the United States (1861–1865)
[2]**Library of Congress:** the national library of the United States, founded in Washington, D.C., in 1800
[3]**candidates:** people who run in an election
[4]**moral values:** beliefs about what is right and wrong

PART A

Circle *T* for true or *F* for false.

T F **1.** The article in Lincoln's pocket criticized his handling of the war.

T F **2.** According to the passage, Lincoln would probably be accepted as a leader today.

T F **3.** According to the passage, today's political candidates—unlike Lincoln—emphasize style more than moral values.

T F **4.** Lincoln found strength by reading newspapers.

T F **5.** According to the passage, today's leaders could learn a lesson from Lincoln and try to be more like him.

PART B

Study the cartoon. Then circle the best answer for the question.

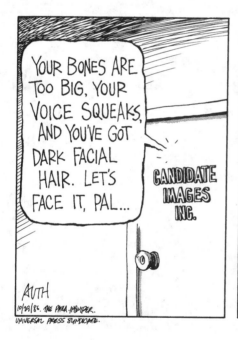

1. What is the main idea of the cartoon?
    (1) Lincoln was a loser.
    (2) Lincoln went to an image specialist.
    (3) Lincoln might not be elected if he were running for president today.
    (4) No bearded man has ever been elected president.

Check your answers on page 190–191.

Exercise 3

Is economic success or political freedom more important? How did two African American leaders value these goals?

Read the passage and complete the exercise.

LANGUAGE Tip

DuBois   doo BOYS

W. E. B. DuBois was born in Massachusetts in 1868. He was the first African American to earn a doctoral degree at Harvard University. His thesis was about the slave trade in America.

Washington and DuBois

Both Booker T. Washington and W. E. B. DuBois wanted to improve the lives of African Americans. Yet they disagreed on how to do it.

In 1895, Booker T. Washington gave a famous speech. He described the path that African Americans should follow: "No race can prosper till it learns that there is as much dignity in tilling a field as in writing a poem. It is at the bottom of life we must begin, not at the top." Washington preached the value of hard work. He urged African Americans to get job training. He said they would be able to improve their economic rank in society if they were educated. Gaining equality was not his chief aim.

W. E. B. DuBois felt that Washington aimed too low. In 1903, DuBois wrote an essay responding to Washington's ideas. To DuBois, Washington's "gospel of Work and Money" seemed "almost completely to **overshadow**[1] the higher aims of life." DuBois, like Washington, thought that economic growth was important. DuBois, however, believed that **segregation**[2] blocked economic growth.

Unlike Washington, DuBois thought African Americans should fight for their civil rights. He said that segregation was blocking their climb toward success. DuBois felt that Washington stressed pleasing whites, and this meant accepting unfair laws.

Booker T. Washington

W. E. B. DuBois

---

[1]**overshadow:** to become more important than
[2]**segregation:** the separation of races, classes, or ethnic groups

1. What issue did both Washington and DuBois address?
    (1) teaching people to write poetry
    (2) making life better for African Americans
    (3) training people for jobs
    (4) farming

2. What goal did both Washington and DuBois think was important?
    (1) achieving economic growth
    (2) ending segregation
    (3) getting along with white people
    (4) accepting unfair laws

3. How did DuBois's views differ from Washington's views?
    (1) DuBois thought earning money was not necessary.
    (2) DuBois felt reaching economic goals did not matter.
    (3) DuBois believed that fighting for civil rights should be a primary goal.
    (4) DuBois thought jobs were more important than politics.

Check your answers on page 191.

 # Writing Workshop

Prewriting
In this chapter, you read about Rosie the Riveter and Condoleezza Rice. Think of two TV characters. Make a chart to show the similarities and differences of these characters.

Drafting
Use your chart to write a paragraph comparing and contrasting the two characters.

Revising
Add clue words that signal comparisons and contrasts, such as *also, in the same way, similar, but, different,* and *however.*

Editing
Be sure that adjectives comparing two things either end in *-er* or use the word *more.* For example: Joan has a more successful career than Maria, but Maria is happier than Joan.

Review – U.S. History

When the United States entered World War II, all people of Japanese descent who were living in the western part of the United States were forced to move. How would you feel if the government forced you to leave your home?

Read the passage. Then circle the best answer for each question.

Japanese Internment in World War II

On December 7, 1941, Japan bombed the U.S. navy base at Pearl Harbor, Hawaii. The next day, the United States declared war on Japan. On February 16, 1942, President Franklin D. Roosevelt signed Executive Order 9066. It gave the military permission to remove all Japanese and Japanese Americans from the West Coast. Their forced move began in April. The people had to leave behind their homes, their jobs, their businesses, and their non-Japanese friends. They were allowed to take only a few possessions.

In 1942, about 110,000 Japanese and Japanese Americans were living on the mainland of the United States. Most were living on the West Coast, from California to Washington. About two-thirds were U.S. citizens. Many of the noncitizens were the parents or grandparents of U.S. citizens.

After the bombing of Pearl Harbor, many Americans feared that Japan would attack the U.S. mainland. Some Americans feared that the Japanese and Japanese Americans on the West Coast would help Japan if an invasion began. They did not trust the loyalty of Japanese Americans. However, there has never been any proof that Japanese Americans were not loyal to the United States.

By April 1942, the U.S. army had set up 10 **internment**[1] camps. The camps were in areas of Arizona, Arkansas, California, Colorado, Idaho, Utah, and Wyoming where few people lived. Some camps were in the mountains. Most camps were in the desert. Barbed wire surrounded the camps, and armed soldiers guarded them. The people lived in **barracks.**[2] Each family had a single room. Everyone ate meals together in big dining halls. There was little private space.

---

[1]**internment:** the confining, or locking up, of people during a war
[2]**barracks:** large buildings that provide a place for people to live

The United States was also at war with Germany and Italy. However, German Americans and Italian Americans were treated differently from Japanese Americans. They were not forced to give up their homes and businesses or to move to internment camps.

1. When did the United States declare war on Japan?
   (1) December 7, 1941
   (2) December 8, 1941
   (3) February 16, 1942
   (4) April 1942

2. Which problem was the government trying to solve by the internment of the Japanese and Japanese Americans?
   (1) Japan's threat to bomb Pearl Harbor
   (2) the U.S. declaration of war against Japan
   (3) Japanese and Japanese Americans in the United States giving aid to Japan
   (4) the military's need for more land

3. How were German Americans treated differently from Japanese Americans?
   (1) German Americans had to give up their businesses but not their homes.
   (2) German Americans had to register so the government knew where they were living.
   (3) German Americans were not allowed to join the military.
   (4) German Americans did not lose their homes or their businesses.

4. What was one effect that the internment had on the Japanese and Japanese Americans?
   (1) Most camps were in the desert.
   (2) They lost almost everything that they had worked all their lives for.
   (3) The camps were surrounded by barbed wire and guarded by soldiers.
   (4) There was little private space in the camps.

Check your answers on page 191.

UNIT 3
Civics and Government

IN THE UNITED STATES, we have national, state, and local governments. All of these governments make laws to protect us. They collect taxes. Then they use that money to pay for schools, bridges, roads, medical care, and much more.

What does the government ask in return? We must obey the law, pay taxes, and appear for jury duty if called. We also have the responsibility to be good citizens. This includes learning about current problems and voting in elections.

After reading this unit, you should be able to

- find facts and opinions
- make inferences
- predict what will happen
- understand political cartoons

Chapter 9

Fact and Opinion

Have you ever read letters to the editor in newspapers and magazines? These letters may state facts. However, the main purpose of the letters is to state the writer's opinion.

A **fact** is a statement that can be proved true. An **opinion** is a statement that tells someone's feelings or beliefs. You may agree or disagree with someone's opinion. Opinions should be based on facts, but they are not facts.

This writer is stating an opinion about the mayor.

> **I think Mayor Joan Harvey is doing a great job. We should reelect her next Tuesday.**

This writer is also stating an opinion, but she is supporting her opinion with facts. You could do research to check that Mayor Harvey did everything mentioned.

> **Mayor Joan Harvey's policies have kept Jones Manufacturing from leaving the city. She worked with the City Council to create three new playgrounds. I think Mayor Harvey is doing a great job. We should reelect her next Tuesday.**

The Rule of Law

The "rule of law" refers to two important ideas. First, everyone in a society has the responsibility to obey a set of laws. Second, all members of the society have the right to know what the laws are. The rule of law in the United States is based on the U.S. Constitution.

The rule of law works well when laws are fair and when they are fairly applied to all members of society.

U.S. Supreme Court building

However, the rule of law has not always worked in the United States. The court case *Plessy versus Ferguson* is an example of a time when the rule of law did not work. The U.S. Supreme Court ruled that African Americans could not ride in the same train car as whites. This ruling was made in 1896. It was the beginning of more than 50 years of discrimination against African Americans. I think that treating people differently because of their race is unfair.

In my opinion, the rule of law works only for people with money and education. These people can hire the best lawyers. No one else ever gets a fair chance in court.

Byron Massie

◆ **Read the following sentences from the passage. Then circle *F* if the statement is a fact or *O* if it is an opinion.**

F   O   **1.** The rule of law in the United States is based on the U.S. Constitution.

F   O   **2.** The rule of law has not always worked in the United States.

F   O   **3.** *Plessy versus Ferguson* was the beginning of more than 50 years of discrimination against African Americans.

F   O   **4.** In my opinion, the rule of law works only for those with money and education.

F   O   **5.** No one else ever gets a fair chance in court.

Here are the answers: 1. F, 2. F, 3. F, 4. O, 5. O

Strategy: How to Identify Facts and Opinions

- Find statements that can be proved true. These are facts.
- Look for clue words that signal opinions. Examples include *I believe, I feel, I think,* and *in my opinion.*
- Words such as *no one, everyone, always, better,* and *worse* may also signal opinions.
- Opinions that are supported by facts are more likely to be accepted by others.

Exercise 1

Have you ever had to give in so people would agree to do something? Were you happy with the results? Did the new plan work?

Read the passage and complete the exercise.

Creating the Plan of Government

The Revolutionary War began in 1775. The next year, delegates from all 13 states came together to write a plan of government for the new nation. By 1787, it was clear that this plan was not working. The states called another meeting. Delegates soon began writing a new plan. They wrote the U.S. Constitution.

Creating the U.S. Constitution required compromises. Each delegate represented the interests of his state. Big states like New York had different needs and wants than small states like Vermont. Southern states had different interests than Northern states. If there was to be an agreement, each state would have to give up a little.

The first compromise was about the kind of government that the nation should have. Some delegates thought that the central government should be strong. Others, however, thought it should be weak. They wanted state governments to have more power than the central government. The delegates compromised and agreed on a federal system. Some powers were given to the national government, and other powers were given to the state governments.

Another compromise was made about representation in Congress. Delegates from large states felt that they should have more seats than small states. Delegates from small states

The signing of the U.S. Constitution

would not agree to this plan. In the end, delegates decided on two houses for Congress. In the House of Representatives, members would be chosen on the basis of state population. However, in the Senate, each state would have two members.

Another difficult issue was slavery. Arguments for and against slavery almost broke apart the new nation. Some states did not support slavery. However, North Carolina, South Carolina, and Georgia demanded that slavery be allowed. The delegates compromised again. They agreed to allow enslaved Africans to be brought into the country until 1808.

The U.S. Constitution was a carefully thought-out plan. In more than 220 years, only 27 changes, or amendments, have been made to it.

PART A

Circle *F* if the statement is a fact and *O* if it is an opinion.

F O **1.** The Constitution replaced an earlier plan of government.

F O **2.** The delegates agreed to a number of compromises.

F O **3.** Large states had the best plan for deciding how many representatives each state would have in Congress.

F O **4.** The delegates were able to work out a plan for representatives in Congress.

F O **5.** Southern states wanted to keep slavery in their states.

F O **6.** The compromise on the slave trade was not a good solution.

PART B

Check (✔) each statement that is a fact.

_____ **(1)** Having a Senate and a House of Representatives satisfied both large and small states.

_____ **(2)** Small states had issues that were different from the issues of large states.

_____ **(3)** Northern states had better ideas than Southern states about how to solve the slavery question.

_____ **(4)** Compromises always work well.

_____ **(5)** Both small and large states sent delegates who wanted to make a plan of government that would work well.

_____ **(6)** The U.S. Constitution is the best constitution in the world.

Check your answers on page 191.

Exercise 2

How can you learn about candidates before an election? How can you find out about the issues?

Read the passage. Then answer the questions.

LANGUAGE *Tip*

Languages change when people need new words to talk about new ideas or new technology. The word *blog* was used for the first time in 1997. It means "a log (diary) on a Web site." Today *blog* is a common word.

The Internet and Political Campaigns

Since the mid-1990s, the Internet has been changing our lives. It has changed the way we communicate. It has changed the way companies do business. Beginning with the 2000 election, it also changed the way we vote for public officials. That year, the people of Arizona became the first people to ever vote online. This, however, is not the biggest change that the Internet has made to elections.

Candidates now use the Internet to manage their campaigns. The Internet has become an important fund-raising tool. People can make donations to political candidates by going online and using their credit cards. In the 2004 election, John Kerry, the Democratic candidate for president, raised $82 million online. Candidates also use the Internet to keep in touch with their supporters. One candidate said that he sent e-mails to 3 million supporters.

Political blogs have also become a part of modern campaigns. Bloggers think they have important things to say about the candidates and the issues. They describe events they have seen or heard about. They may post new information several times a day. They give links to other Web sites with interesting information. Some people write blogs just because they like politics. Some reporters write blogs. Campaigns may hire bloggers to be on their staff. Candidates want to be sure that people get frequent reports about what is happening in the campaign.

Bloggers often try to be the first to write about breaking news. This means that bloggers may not know the full story when they put information on the Internet. Many bloggers write about only one candidate or one political party. They let their personal opinions affect everything they say. If you want opinions, blogs may be a good place to look. However, if you want facts, go to a different source.

1. Which statement is *not* a fact about how the Internet is changing elections?
   (1) Candidates raise money on the Internet.
   (2) Newspaper reporters sometimes write blogs on the Internet.
   (3) Blogs are the best source for up-to-date information.
   (4) Regular e-mails keep a candidate in touch with supporters.

2. Which statement is an opinion most bloggers are likely to agree with?
   (1) The Internet should contain only facts.
   (2) Bloggers have important information that others should read.
   (3) Millions of people read blogs every day.
   (4) Blogs written by reporters are better than blogs written by campaign staff members.

3. Which sentence is an opinion about using the Internet in political campaigns?
   (1) Many candidates use the Internet to send e-mails to their supporters.
   (2) The Internet is the best way for a candidate to raise money.
   (3) The Internet has changed some of the ways that candidates campaign.
   (4) Fund-raising online can bring in huge sums of money for candidates.

4. What is one problem with bloggers?
   (1) They have interesting ideas.
   (2) They may be newspaper reporters.
   (3) They encourage people to vote online.
   (4) They may not take time to learn all the facts.

Check your answers on page 191.

Women could not vote in most states until 1920. What other groups of people have not been able to vote in the United States?

Read the passage. Then circle the best answer for each question.

Extending Voting Rights

The U.S. government has only a few requirements about who can vote. Voters must be U.S. citizens. They must be at least 18 years of age. They must be registered to vote. They must live in the district where they are voting. There are no other requirements. However, this has not always been true.

Before the Civil War, women and African Americans were not allowed to vote. In 1870, the 15th Amendment gave African American men the right to vote. Women—both white and African American—thought they would get the right to vote at the same time. Instead, they had to wait another 50 years. The 19th Amendment, which gave women the right to vote, was ratified (or approved) in 1920.

Why had women not been allowed to vote? Several arguments were commonly made. First, many people thought that women were supposed to take care of the home and family. Everything else belonged to men. Therefore, politics was for men, not women. Second, many men believed that women were not smart enough to understand politics. Third, some people thought that women were too good to become involved in politics. However, others believed that good women would make politics more honest.

By 1915, women in 11 Western states could vote in local elections. They could not, however, vote for president. Why did Eastern and Southern states not have laws that were similar to laws in the West? Men in the West thought of women as their equals. Life was hard in the West. Women and men had to work together to succeed. They worked their farms together, and they raised their families together. They built their towns together. In the East and South, men thought it was their job to take care of women.

From the time the U.S. Constitution was written until 1971, the voting age in the United States was 21. People under 21 years of age were not considered adult enough to make good decisions. But by the late 1960s, thousands of young Americans were fighting in Vietnam. Many young people wanted to vote. They had a strong argument. If they were old enough to fight—and die—for their country, they were old enough to vote. The 26th Amendment, which gave 18-year-olds the right to vote, became law in 1971.

It is important that U.S. citizens protect their right to vote. The best way to do this is by voting!

Circle *F* if the statement is a fact and *O* if it is an opinion.

F   O   **1.** There are few requirements for voters in the United States.

F   O   **2.** Young adults deserved the right to vote.

F   O   **3.** Only men are smart enough to vote.

F   O   **4.** If women voted, they would forget their duties to their home and family.

F   O   **5.** The attitude of men in the East and South toward women was different from the attitude of men in the West.

F   O   **6.** Some people said women were too good to vote.

Check your answers on page 191.

Writing Workshop

Prewriting
In this chapter, you learned that letters to the editor usually express the writer's opinion about a problem. Make a list of problems in your community such as the high cost of riding the bus, the need for more traffic lights, or the lack of evening classes for adults. Choose one topic. Then brainstorm to list ideas about this topic.

Drafting
Write a letter to the editor of your local newspaper about this topic. State your main idea in the opening sentence. Use some of the ideas in your list as the details. Make your argument stronger by including facts.

Revising
Check each fact to be sure it is correct. When possible, tell where you found your facts. For example, "The mayor's Web site reports that . . ."

Editing
Check your letter for the correct use of commas in dates and addresses. Use commas between

the day and the year	March 12, 2010
the day of the week and the date	Sunday, June 3
the city and state	Yonkers, New York

Chapter 10

Inferences

You have a plan to turn an empty lot into a community garden. You have lined up support in your neighborhood. People are willing to clean up the lot. Six families want to plant gardens. The problem is the city. Your project needs a license. After you explain your idea to your city councilwoman, she says, "I am very impressed with your plan. I have to take your idea to the city council, but projects like this are what we like to see."

What do the councilwoman's comments suggest? Can you "read between the lines"? The councilwoman does not directly say, "The council will approve your plan." However, she hints that there is a good chance your plan will be approved. Using clues to figure out what someone is suggesting is called **making an inference**.

Try your skill at making an inference. The zoning board is deciding whether to approve a new shopping mall. People are marching outside the hearing room. Some want the shopping mall, and some do not. People are carrying these signs.

A	B
NO More Traffic!	More Stores Bring Tax Dollars for the City
More Traffic = More Pollution	New Mall = More Jobs
Chain Stores Kill Local Stores	More Businesses Mean More Choices

Which column lists signs carried by people who

(1) want the mall? _____   (2) do not want the mall? _____

People carrying the signs listed in **column B want the mall**. People carrying the signs listed in **column A do not want the mall**.

As you read the following passage, look for clues that tell you what the author really wants you to understand.

Stop and Frisk

The 4th Amendment to the U.S. Constitution protects people from "unreasonable searches and **seizures**."[1] It also states that a judge can issue a search warrant. A search warrant allows police to search someone. However, no judge can issue a

---

[1] **seizures:** the taking away of property

search warrant unless there is "probable cause." The police must have reason to believe that a person or place has been involved in a crime.

However, police officers may conduct some searches without a warrant. One search done without a warrant is called "stop and frisk." The person who is stopped must have been acting suspiciously. The police must think the person is likely to be carrying a weapon. Illegal substances found during a street stop may be taken away. The officer must be able to tell that something is illegal by the way it feels.

How does a police officer decide who looks suspicious? Many people think young African American or Hispanic men are stopped and searched more often than other people. A branch of the American Civil Liberties Union and the lawyers' association in one state decided to find out. They filed a lawsuit against the police department of the state's biggest city. They wanted to see the records on stop-and-frisk actions. They wanted to compare the number of white and nonwhite street stops.

The police department, however, refused to share its records. The department claimed that its officers do not do **racial profiling**.[2] If the police department would not share information, you might ask, "What are the police hiding?" Perhaps they do not want anyone to know how many white men have been stopped and searched.

---

[2]**racial profiling:** treating people unfairly because of their race

◆ The author's opinion about stop-and-frisk actions is not directly stated in the passage. Write two sentences from the passage that suggest what the author thinks about street stops.

_____

Here are clues in the passage: If the police department would not share information, you might ask, "What are they hiding?" *and* Perhaps they do not want anyone to know how many white men have been stopped and searched.

Strategy: How to Make Inferences

- Identify the topic, main idea, and details.
- Figure out why the author included certain details.
- Read between the lines. What do the details suggest?

Exercise 1

Have you ever thought of volunteering to work for a political candidate? What skills could you offer? How much time could you give?

Read the passage. Then answer the questions.

Getting Involved in Politics

One responsibility of a citizen is to be an informed voter. Before we vote, we need to understand the issues. We also need to learn about candidates' views on these issues. Then we can decide which candidates to support.

If we have a little time, we can do more than that. We can work for the election of the candidates that we support. It does not take much time to talk to friends and family about candidates. It takes only seconds to pin campaign buttons on our coats or put bumper stickers on our cars.

If we have more time, we can volunteer to work for a campaign. Campaigns need volunteers to do all kinds of jobs. Volunteers put address labels on campaign brochures. They stuff envelopes with letters about the candidate. They make telephone calls to tell voters about the candidate. Campaign leaders prepare a script for volunteers to read over the phone. Volunteers may also go door to door talking to voters. They hand out campaign literature and ask people to vote for their candidate. Again, the campaign suggests what volunteers should talk about.

The work of volunteers does not end when the polls open. On election day, volunteers may call voters and remind them to vote. They may drive older voters and voters with disabilities to the polls.

Some volunteers find they like politics so much that they decide to become paid campaign workers. People are hired to be campaign managers, press secretaries, organizers, and pollsters. An organizer sets up the campaign office and recruits volunteers. A pollster is an expert at taking public-opinion polls. He or she advises the candidate about issues that are important to voters. People choose politics as a career for a number of reasons. The most important reason is to help elect the best possible people to run our government.

Circle the best answer for each question.

1. What do you think the writer's viewpoint is about political campaigns?
   (1) They are important some years.
   (2) They are important only to volunteers.
   (3) They are always important.
   (4) They are not important.

2. What does the writer suggest about the skills that volunteers need?
   (1) Volunteers can be useful even if they have only a little time.
   (2) Volunteers are told exactly how to do each job.
   (3) No skills are needed to do volunteer jobs.
   (4) There are various jobs that require a variety of skills.

3. What can you infer about why scripts are written for volunteers to use when they talk to voters?
   (1) No volunteer actually uses the script.
   (2) Scripts help volunteers say the most important things about the candidate.
   (3) Most volunteers write their own scripts.
   (4) Writing the script gives a volunteer something to do.

4. What can you infer about giving time to help a candidate win an election?
   (1) It takes a great amount of time.
   (2) People can give as much or as little time as they want.
   (3) Giving time is more important than giving money.
   (4) Only full-time paid workers make a difference.

5. Check (✔) all the jobs done by campaign volunteers.
   _____ (1) address envelopes for mailing campaign literature
   _____ (2) take elderly voters to the polls on election day
   _____ (3) take public-opinion polls
   _____ (4) remind people to vote
   _____ (5) set up a candidate's campaign office

Check your answers on page 192.

Exercise 2

Have you ever wondered what your tax dollars pay for? How would our lives be different if government had less money to spend?

Read the passage. Then answer the questions.

What Taxes Pay For

Federal, state, and local governments collect taxes to pay their bills. There are various kinds of taxes. Individuals and companies pay income taxes. People pay sales taxes in most states and many cities. Drivers pay gasoline taxes. Smokers pay taxes on cigarettes. If you have electrical work done in your house, you may need to pay for a permit. This permit is a form of tax. A dog license is another form of tax.

Most people complain about paying taxes. Many politicians make campaign promises to cut taxes. But what would happen if we did not pay taxes?

The federal government makes laws about what it will tax. It also makes laws about how it will spend tax money. Federal taxes pay for programs such as Social Security, Medicare, and food stamps. These programs help older Americans and people who are in need. In addition, the federal government has thousands of federal programs that benefit us every day. Here are a few examples:

- The Department of Transportation builds and repairs roads and bridges. It enforces airline and railroad safety.
- The Environmental Protection Agency enforces laws that help keep our air and water clean. It recommends fuel standards for cars, trucks, and buses.

- The Department of Health and Human Services pays for HIV/AIDS and cancer research. It checks the safety of food, drugs, clothing, and toys.
- The Department of Labor enforces safe working conditions and minimum-wage laws. It operates job-training programs.

City taxes have other purposes. These taxes pay for schools, libraries, and parks. They are used to repair city streets and put up traffic lights. They also pay the salaries of police, fire fighters, and city planners.

Paying taxes is one way that citizens take part in government. Using government services is another way.

1. What is the main idea of this passage?
   (1) All levels of government collect taxes.
   (2) More services could be provided if people paid higher taxes.
   (3) Taxes should be cut.
   (4) Taxes pay for services that benefit us all.

2. What can you infer about the writer's opinion about taxes?
   (1) Taxes are too high, and they should be cut.
   (2) Taxes are important because they pay for needed services.
   (3) Taxes help only certain groups.
   (4) The writer has no opinion about taxes.

3. What can you infer about which programs are most likely to be paid for by federal tax money?
   (1) programs that are very expensive
   (2) programs suggested by the president
   (3) programs that benefit people all over the United States
   (4) programs that cities do not have enough money to pay for

4. Check (✔) all the expenses that would be paid for by the federal government.
   _____ (1) building new sidewalks
   _____ (2) planning space flights
   _____ (3) paying members of Congress
   _____ (4) buying a statue for a city park
   _____ (5) hiring Peace Corps volunteers

Check your answers on page 192.

Exercise 3

Do you know that most government business is public? This is the law. What information about your city or state government would you like to know?

Read the passage and complete the exercise.

Sunshine Laws

Abraham Lincoln said that the U.S. government is "of the people, by the people, and for the people." He meant that the people created the government, they control the government, and they are served by the government. U.S. citizens have the right to know what is going on in government.

To protect this right, "sunshine laws" have been written. These laws require that all government activities are carried out in daylight—that is, that they be carried out where citizens can see what is happening. Sunshine laws require that government meetings be open to the public. They also require that records of these meetings are public. (Discussions about employees and their salaries are usually not covered by sunshine laws.)

Most states have sunshine laws. These laws apply to state, county, and city governments. Florida's sunshine law is a good example. It requires that meetings of public boards are open to the public. The place and time of these meetings must be announced in advance. Minutes must be taken at all meetings. Florida's sunshine law applies whenever two or more public officials are discussing public issues in person, by phone, or on e-mail.

Because of sunshine laws, people can look at the records of public agencies. They can read the reports of the state board of education as well as minutes of a city council meeting. Most police reports, court actions, wills, bankruptcies, building permits, and donations to election campaigns are public information.

The federal government has its own sunshine law. In 1976, Congress passed the Freedom of Information Act. It gives people the right to look at federal records. They can check on whether the FBI has a file on them, and they can look at that file. People can read contracts made by the federal government with companies in their area. The salaries of federal workers are also public information. The purpose of all sunshine laws is to be sure that government is serving all citizens fairly.

1. What clue in the passage tells you that the writer thinks sunshine laws are a good idea?

   Clue: _____

2. What clue tells you that most state sunshine laws are similar to Florida's law?

   Clue: _____

3. What inference can you make about how sunshine laws help make good government?

   _____

Check your answers on page 192.

Writing Workshop

Prewriting
Watch a TV news program where people discuss political issues. Listen closely to the statements that people make. Take notes on their comments. Highlight (or underline) the most important points of the discussion.

Drafting
Write a paragraph stating the view of one speaker on the news program you watched. Include quotations from the speaker. Then make an inference about the person's point of view.

Revising
Read your paragraph to a partner. Ask the partner whether you have given enough details so your inference seems logical. If your partner does not understand how you made the inference, add more details so the speaker's ideas are more clear.

Editing
Check that you have used quotation marks only when you have used the exact words of the speaker.

> The senator said, "I support higher gas taxes."
> The senator said that he was going to vote for higher taxes.

Chapter 11

Predicting

Before you watch a football game, do you predict who the winner will be? Sports announcers often do. They look at the strengths and the weaknesses of each team. They think about the coaches and the key players. They also review each team's win–loss record. Then sports announcers predict the outcome of the game.

Predicting means figuring out what will happen. You probably make predictions as you read stories or watch movies. You can also make predictions as you read social studies passages. As you read, combine what you know about how people usually act with information in the passage. Then make a prediction about what will happen next. As you read on, see if your prediction is correct. Making predictions as you read helps you watch for details. It also helps you think about how events are related.

In politics, polling is one way to predict an outcome. **Polls** are surveys of people's opinions. During an election year, polls are often in the news. They report voters' views of the candidates and the issues. The information in the polls provides clues about the future. These clues are used to predict what might happen: Who will win the election? Which political party will control Congress? Who will the new mayor be?

As you read the following passage, look for clues that will help you make a prediction.

The Future of Women in Politics

Women did not get the right to vote until 1920. However, women have become an important force in U.S. politics. After the election of November 2006, 16 women were serving in the U.S. Senate, and 70 women were serving in the House of Representatives. Eight states had women governors. At that time, Senator Hillary Clinton was a leading Democratic candidate for president in the 2008 election.

Hillary Rodham Clinton

Politicians understand that they must win the support of women voters. They know that more women than men have voted in every election since 1964.

Surveys show these facts about women voters:

- They want government to provide more services.
- They want the United States to stay out of wars.
- They want government to play a more important role in health care.
- They want more gun control.

Today women serve as mayors, governors, members of Congress, and members of the president's cabinet. Their numbers are expected to grow in future elections.

◆ **Answer this question in the space provided.**

Why are politicians interested in the opinions of women?

_____

You are correct if you wrote **more women vote than men.**

◆ **Now it is your turn to predict an outcome. Use information in the passage to make a prediction about women's future in politics.**

_____

Perhaps you wrote **more women will run for public office.** The results of polls and surveys show this is a likely outcome.

Strategy: How to Predict

- Think about what you already know about the topic.
- Notice clues that the author gives you. What facts are given? Does the author explain causes and effects?
- Use this information to figure out what might happen.

Exercise 1

Why is it important to get a good education? How can the lack of education hurt a person's future?

Read the passage and answer the questions.

Civil Rights and Education

Getting an education was an important goal for African Americans after the Civil War ended in 1865. It became more difficult to reach this goal after 1896. In that year, the U.S. Supreme Court established the "separate but equal" rule. African Americans and whites could be separated as long as the **facilities**[1] were equal. For example, the railroad car used by African Americans had to be as good as the railroad car used by whites. The separate-but-equal rule was later applied to schools.

However, the **segregated**[2] schools were not equal. Beginning in the 1930s, African Americans began to bring lawsuits. They wanted to open all schools to African Americans. First, they sued universities for refusing to accept African American students. The African Americans won. Then they sued school districts. Finally, in 1954 the National Association for the Advancement of Colored People (NAACP) sued the school district of Topeka, Kansas. It sued on behalf of eight-year-old Linda Brown. She was not allowed to go to the school in her neighborhood. Instead, she had to go to an all-black school across town.

The lawsuit went all the way to the U.S. Supreme Court. The Court ruled that the Kansas law was unconstitutional. The Court ruling meant that similar laws in other cities were also unconstitutional. In 1955, the Court

Eight-year-old Linda Brown

---

[1]**facilities:** places such as movie theaters, hotels, and restaurants

[2]**segregated:** separate, kept apart

said that all states had to begin to **desegregate**[3] their school systems. They had to do so "with all **deliberate**[4] speed." This was true for both Northern and Southern states. Civil rights leaders did not expect that it would be easy to follow this ruling.

Not all states and school districts obeyed. Most Southern states resisted. Some districts allowed private schools for white students to open. Other districts simply refused to obey. By 1969, the Supreme Court ruled that segregated schools had to end immediately. The time for "deliberate speed" was over.

[3]**desegregate:** end the separation of races
[4]**deliberate:** planned

1. What was the outcome of the court case against the Topeka school district?

   _____

2. What did civil rights leaders predict about ending segregated schools?

   _____

3. Write one fact that proves the prediction of the civil rights leaders to be accurate.

   _____

   _____

4. What can you predict about the education that African Americans received after schools were desegregated?

   _____

   _____

Check your answers on page 192.

Exercise 2

Do you think of yourself as a Republican, a Democrat, or an independent? What do you like about the two main political parties? What do you dislike about them?

Read the passage. Then circle the best answer for each question.

LANGUAGE Tip

Sometimes a **third-party** candidate runs for office. The Green Party, the Reform Party, and the Socialist Party are some of the "third parties" that have supported a candidate for president.

Republican, Democrat, or Independent?

The purpose of a political party is to help candidates win elections. A political party is made up of people who generally agree on what government should do. They also generally agree on how to do it.

What causes a person to choose one party over the other? There are nine characteristics that affect which party a person chooses. These characteristics are job, income, education, gender, age, religious and ethnic background, geography, friends, and family.

Business leaders and people with higher incomes tend to be Republicans. Union members, women, and younger voters tend to be Democrats. Catholics, African Americans, Hispanics, and new citizens tend to vote Democratic also.

People who live in the South and in certain Midwestern states tend to be Republicans. Big city voters tend to be Democrats.

People often pick friends who feel the same way they do about political issues. As a result, friends tend to vote alike. The single biggest factor, however, is family. People most often belong to the same party their parents belong to.

Independents, on the other hand, do not belong to a political party. They see candidates and policies they do not like in both major parties. They also see ideas they like in both parties. As a result, independents vote for some Democrats and some Republicans.

Since the 1970s, the number of people calling themselves independents has greatly increased. This is an important change in politics. Experts think that 35 percent of voters may be independents. More young people tend to be independents. The number of independents seems to be growing.

1. Which characteristic is most likely to determine the party that a person belongs to?
   (1) education
   (2) friends
   (3) income
   (4) family

2. Which of the following voters would most likely be a Democrat?
   (1) a male doctor in his 50s
   (2) a woman who lives in a big city
   (3) a woman who grew up in a family that voted Republican
   (4) a farmer in Georgia

3. Which of the following voters would most likely be a Republican?
   (1) a bank president
   (2) someone who belongs to a labor union
   (3) a college student
   (4) someone who lives in Philadelphia

4. Why do people call themselves independents?
   (1) They do not like the ideas of the two major parties.
   (2) They do not want to tell which party they support.
   (3) They like some candidates and some ideas in both parties.
   (4) They are very interested in politics.

5. According to the passage, which prediction is mostly likely to be accurate?
   (1) There will be more Democrats in the future.
   (2) There will be more Republicans in the future.
   (3) There will be more independents in the future.
   (4) There will be about the same number of independents in the future.

Check your answers on page 192.

Exercise 3

How do you settle disagreements with family or friends over where to go or what to do? Does one person usually get his or her way? Would that system work in government?

Read the passage and answer the questions.

LANGUAGE Tip

The **Senate** has 100 members.
　Majority: 51 members
　Two-thirds: 67 members
The **House of Representatives** has 435 members.
　Majority: 218 members
　Two-thirds: 290 members

When the President and Congress Disagree

To make a new law, both houses of Congress must write similar bills. Then a majority—that is, at least one more than half—of the members of each house must vote for the bill. Next, the bill is sent to the president. If the president signs the bill within ten days, it becomes a law. However, the president may disagree with a bill. Then he uses his power of veto. When he vetoes a bill, he stops it from becoming a law.

President J. F. Kennedy signing a bill into law

If Congress is in session, the president sends the bill back to the House and the Senate. Congress can do one of two things. It can change the bill so the president will sign it. Or Congress can try to override the veto. This means Congress tries to pass the bill a second time. To override a veto, at least two-thirds of the members of each house must vote for the bill.

Congress often sends bills to the president just before it **adjourns**. If the president disagrees with one of these bills, he can use a pocket veto. The president puts the bill aside. He does not sign it. Because Congress is not in session, he cannot send it back to be changed or to be passed again. The bill does not become a law.

A veto is a strong message to Congress. Sometimes Congress will decide not to pass a bill because the president has said he will veto it. This was a tool that President George W. Bush often used. He did not veto a bill until his second term. Franklin Roosevelt vetoed 635 bills. Congress was able to override only two of Roosevelt's vetoes. Since the 1960s, most presidents have vetoed fewer than 40 bills. Congress usually cannot override a veto.

Sometimes Congress passes a bill even though the president has threatened to veto it. In 2007, Congress passed a water projects bill for $23 billion. President Bush

---

adjourns: ends a meeting

had threatened to veto this bill. He said the water projects cost too much money. However, the bill was popular with Congress and with the public. More than two-thirds of the members of each house had passed the bill. When the President vetoed it, experts predicted that Congress would override his veto. The experts were right.

1. Why does a president veto a bill?_____

2. How can Congress override a president's veto?_____

3. Why did experts predict that Congress would override President Bush's veto of the 2007

   water projects bill?_____

4. What is a pocket veto?_____

   _____

Check your answers on page 192.

Writing Workshop

Prewriting
In this chapter, you read the results of surveys about women in politics. Write a list of questions you would like to ask in a political survey. Then find three questions related to one topic, such as taxes or immigration. Ask your friends these questions.

Drafting
Write a paragraph that summarizes the responses to your survey. At the end of the paragraph, include a sentence that makes a prediction.

Revising
Fix a run-on sentence by making it into two (or more) shorter sentences. You can also join the two sentences with *and, but, yet,* or *or.*

Editing
Check that you have capitalized the names of all people and places. If a name has more than one word, all the important words are capitalized. Example: Statue of Liberty.

Chapter 12

Political Cartoons

Artists draw cartoons to make us laugh. What the characters do and what they say may also give us something to think about.

Political cartoons are about current events. Their main purpose is to make us think. However, they may also make us laugh.

Through pictures and words, political cartoonists state an opinion. Each political cartoon has a point of view. The characters and objects in political cartoons may be symbols. A **symbol** stands for or represents something else. Uncle Sam, the elephant, and the donkey appear in many political cartoons.

Study this political cartoon. First, read the background notes. They tell you about details in the cartoon. Then read the labels on the car and the trucks. Notice the words that the characters are saying.

The Economy

Background notes: People in the United States are concerned about how government policy affects the economy. The economy is usually a key issue in elections.

- The elephant is the symbol of the Republican Party.
- "G.O.P." stands for Grand Old Party. This is another name for the Republican Party.
- The donkey is the symbol of the Democratic Party.
- "DEM." means Democrats.
- The man is Uncle Sam. He is a symbol of the United States. He always has white hair and a beard, and he wears a top hat.

◆ Describe what is happening in the cartoon.

1. What kind of trucks are the Democratic Party and the Republican Party driving?

_____

2. What is wrong with the car labeled "U.S. economy"?

_____

3. What are the two political parties trying to do?

_____

4. What can you infer from what the characters are saying?

_____

5. Why does the cartoonist have the "DEM." and the "G.O.P." saying the same words?

_____

Here are the answers to the questions:

1. They are driving tow trucks.
2. The car (the economy) is falling apart.
3. They are trying to tow the car in opposite directions.
4. Both parties think they can fix the economy quickly.
5. Both parties claim they can solve a problem, but their solutions are usually different.

Understanding political cartoons is like putting together the pieces of a puzzle. All the parts must be added together to find the meaning of the cartoon.

Strategy: How to Understand Political Cartoons

- Look at the characters. Who are they? What are they saying?
- Read every word in the cartoon. Study the labels and descriptions.
- Are there any symbols in the cartoon? What do the symbols stand for?
- Use the details to infer the cartoonist's point of view.

Exercise 1

Why are medical bills so high? Do you think the government needs to change the health care system?

Read the background notes and study the political cartoon. Then answer the questions.

The Politics of Health Care

Background notes: Health care costs keep rising. The cost of doctors' visits, drugs, and medical tests go up every year. Many people cannot afford to see a doctor because they cannot afford health insurance. More than 45 million Americans are uninsured. Many of them are children. The federal and state governments have cut Medicaid funding for the poor.

Some people think we could have a better health care system if the federal government would control health care costs. Then Americans would be able to afford medical care. Other people disagree. No one has been able to solve the problem. As a result, health care continues to be a major issue in elections.

1. Why do some people believe the government should control health care costs?

   _____

   _____

2. Why can't some people afford to see a doctor?

   _____

3. Who does the man in the wheelchair represent?

   _____

4. What does the word *cutbacks* mean?

   _____

5. What have the two men in suits done to the wheelchair?

   _____

6. How is the man in the wheelchair affected by having no wheels?

   _____

7. What might happen to poor people who lose government aid for health care? Base your prediction on the details in the cartoon.

   _____

   _____

Check your answers on page 193.

Exercise 2

Why do people, businesses, and organizations give money to political candidates? What problems might be created if a candidate received large sums of money from a few people, businesses, and organizations?

Read the background notes and study the political cartoon. Then answer the questions.

Campaigning for President

Background notes: Beginning in 1971, Congress passed a number of campaign finance laws. These laws control contributions made to candidates who are running for federal offices. They limit the amount of money that individuals and businesses can give to one candidate. Candidates for federal offices can still raise millions of dollars for their campaigns. The candidates that raise the most money are those running for president.

ST. LOUIS POST-DISPATCH

To try to end this race for money, Congress set up the Presidential Election Campaign Fund. The money in this fund comes from the public. By checking a special box on their tax returns, taxpayers agree to give $3 of their tax payment to this campaign fund. Each candidate in 2008 was offered $84 million. Candidates can refuse the money and raise all the money they need on their own. However, they still must obey the campaign finance laws.

In 2008, Senator Hillary Clinton from New York and Senator Barack Obama from Illinois were running against each other. They both wanted to be the candidate that the Democratic Party would nominate to run for president. Clinton and Obama both refused money from the Presidential Election Campaign Fund. They each raised much more than $150 million in their race to be the Democratic candidate for president.

1. What are the names on the sides of the two trucks?

   _____

2. What is the label on the car?

   _____

3. Who are the drivers of the trucks and the car?

   _____

4. What is happening on the top of each truck?

   _____

5. What do you think the closed container on the top of the car means?

   _____

6. What do you think may happen to the car?

   _____

7. Do you think that the cartoonist approves or disapproves of the candidates' refusing public
   financing for their campaigns? Explain.

   _____

   _____

Check your answers on page 193.

Exercise 3

What do you know about the founding of the nation of Israel? Why is there so much fighting between Israel and the Arab nations?

Read the background notes and study the political cartoon. Then answer the questions.

LANGUAGE Tip

From 1948 to 1966, the city of Jerusalem was divided into two parts. One part belonged to Israel. The other part belonged to Jordan. Jerusalem is a holy city for Christians, Moslems, and Jews.

Problems in the Middle East

Background notes: In 1948, the country of Israel was founded. Israel is located in the Middle East. Many of the people living in the new country were Jews who had left Europe in the 1940s. Arabs in the area believed that the land belonged to them because they had been living there. They called the area Palestine.

War broke out almost immediately. The Israelis won. More wars and fighting have occurred since 1948. Israel has fought not only against Arab nations but also against political groups that represent the Palestinians. One of these groups is HAMAS. It has fought in parts of Israel for many years.

The phrase "between a rock and a hard place" is an idiom, or familiar saying. The six-pointed star is the Star of David. It symbolizes Israel and Jews. The bird is supposed to be a dove, and the leaves represent an olive branch. Both a dove and an olive branch are symbols for peace.

BETWEEN A ROCK AND A HARD PLACE...

1. What do you think the saying "between a rock and a hard place" means?

_____

2. What do the two rocks stand for? _____

3. What is caught between the two rocks?

_____

4. What can you infer about the cartoonist's point of view about peace in the Middle East?

_____

Check your answers on page 193.

Writing Workshop

Prewriting
Find a political cartoon in the newspaper. Make a list of details in the cartoon. Then write notes about what the details mean. Finally, write a title for the cartoon if it does not already have one.

Drafting
Organize your list of details into a paragraph. Your paragraph should create a "word picture" of the cartoon. Use your notes to help explain the meaning of the cartoon.

Revising
Be sure you have organized the details in a logical way. You may describe the details from left to right or top to bottom.

Editing
Check that you have correctly capitalized the words in the title. Capitalize the first word, the last word, and all important words in a title. Example: Working for a Better World Is Important.

Review — Civics and Government

What is global warming? What problems may global warming cause?

Read the passage. Then circle the best answer for each question.

One Effect of Global Warming

Global warming is the rise of Earth's temperatures. Most scientists believe that global warming is caused by human activity. Driving cars, especially those that are not fuel-efficient, is one way to increase global warming. Using coal to produce the power that runs factories is another.

What will happen to planet Earth if global warming continues? Scientists predict that the polar ice caps will melt. The level of the world's oceans will rise. If this happens, the land along the coasts will flood. People will lose their homes and jobs.

People are not the only ones who will be affected. Many animals will also suffer. The U.S. government released a report recently about the polar bear population. It said that two-thirds of the world's polar bears will disappear by the year 2050.

Polar bears live on the Arctic ice cap. Global warming is melting the ice cap. Scientists predict that 40 percent of the ice cap will be gone by the year 2050. As a result, Alaska's polar bear population will die out. Polar bears will be able to live only near Greenland and on some islands near the Arctic ice cap.

Many nations have been working to slow down global warming. They want to change what humans are doing to Earth. One result of their work is the Kyoto Treaty. President George W. Bush refused to sign the treaty. He believed that it would cost U.S. businesses too much money to make the changes ordered by the treaty. However, most other nations have signed the treaty. They feel that the future of planet Earth is worth the price. However, even the nations that signed the treaty have been slow to make changes. Global warming continues.

PART A

1. What can you infer about the effects of global warming?
   (1) Global warming is a problem only for animals.
   (2) Global warming will continue no matter what people do.
   (3) Changing how humans act can affect global warming.
   (4) Most nations of the world are not concerned about global warming.

2. Which statement is an opinion?
   (1) About 40 percent of the Arctic ice cap will disappear by the year 2050.
   (2) The Kyoto Treaty is an effort to reduce global warming.
   (3) Polar bears live on the polar ice cap.
   (4) According to President Bush, the Kyoto Treaty would hurt U.S. businesses.

3. According to the passage, what will happen if global warming continues?
   (1) People will continue to drive cars that are not fuel-efficient.
   (2) People and animals will be affected.
   (3) Nations will not change enough to slow global warming.
   (4) The United States may sign the Kyoto Treaty.

PART B

Look at the political cartoon. Then circle the best answer for each question.

"THEY STARTED HANGING OUT AFTER THE POLE MELTED"

1. Why do you think the polar bears are wearing sunglasses?
   (1) Wearing shades is "cool," and polar bears are supposed to look "cool."
   (2) Sunglasses represent how bright and hot the Sun is because of global warming.
   (3) Polar bears will need to change their habits if they move away from the Arctic.
   (4) The sunglasses have no meaning in this cartoon.

2. Which idea from the passage does this political cartoon help you understand?
   (1) Global warming is being caused by human activity.
   (2) Land along the coasts will flood.
   (3) Global warming is melting the polar ice cap.
   (4) Most other nations have signed the Kyoto Treaty.

Check your answers on page 193.

UNIT 4

Geography

GEOGRAPHY IS THE study of places around the world. It looks at the relationship people have with the part of the world they live in.

Geographers work with a variety of maps. A map is a drawing of a place. The drawing shows where things are located. Maps help you understand geography. By reading maps, you can explore areas of the world you have never visited. Maps can also give you special information. They may show physical features, population patterns, borders between countries or states, or weather patterns.

In this unit, you will learn how to read symbols used on maps. You will also learn how to identify direction and distance on a map. These skills will help you understand the information presented on maps.

Chapter	What You Will Learn About	What You Will Read
13	Map Keys	Reading Around the World U.S. Weather Map Where People Live Native American Lands
14	Finding Directions and Distances	Routes to O'Hare International Airport Main Routes of Migrant Workers The Monsoons in India The Freedom Ride
15	Historical Maps	Early Settlers: 1820–1920 Women's Voting Rights: 1914 Colonies on the African Continent California Missions: 1769–1848
Review	Geography	Moving People and Cattle

After reading this unit, you should be able to

- use a map key

- find distances and directions on a map

- understand historical maps

Chapter 13

Map Keys

A **symbol** is a picture or a design that stands for something. Every day you see symbols that give you information.

Map symbols are a kind of language. Map symbols include pictures, colors, patterns, or shapes that have special meaning on a map. A **map key**, or **legend**, explains the meaning of the symbols.

Look at these maps. Study the map key. It indicates that various shades of color stand for the percentage (%) of adults who cannot read.

Reading Around the World

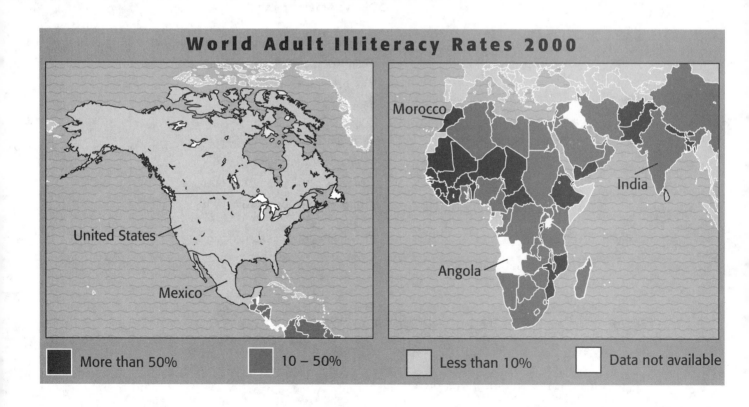

World Adult Illiteracy Rates 2000

United States

Mexico

Morocco

India

Angola

■ More than 50%   ■ 10 – 50%   ☐ Less than 10%   ☐ Data not available

◆ Fill out this chart, using information from the maps.

Country	% of Adults Who Cannot Read
United States	10% or less
India	
Angola	
Morocco	
Mexico	

Here are the answers:

In India, 10%–50% of adults cannot read.

No information (data) is available about Angola.

In Morocco, more than 50% of adults cannot read.

In Mexico, less than 10% of adults cannot read.

Strategy: How to Use a Map Key

- Study the symbols in the map key. What does each symbol represent?
- Find the symbols on the map.
- Think about the information that is explained on the map.

Exercise 1

How does weather affect your daily life? What useful information can you find on a weather map?

Use the map and the background notes to answer the questions.

U.S. Weather Map

Background notes: Many newspapers print a weather map every day. These maps show the expected high and low temperatures in major U.S. cities. The key on the weather map helps you understand weather patterns across the country.

Weather Conditions in the United States

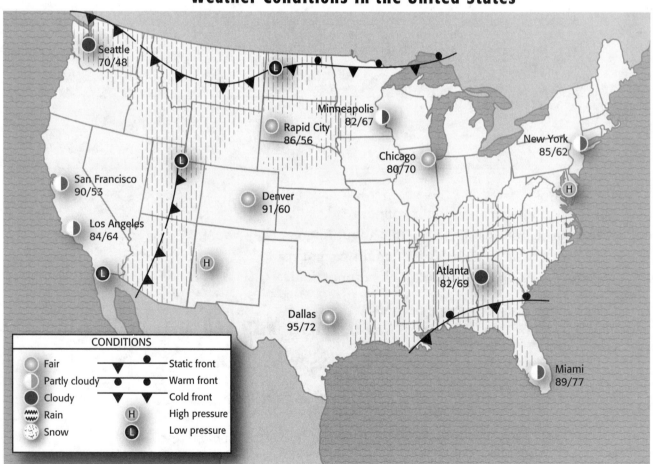

1. Which cities have fair skies?

   _____   _____

   _____   _____

2. Which cities have partly cloudy skies?

   _____   _____

   _____   _____

   _____

3. Which cities have cloudy skies?

   _____   _____

4. Which cities are located closest to a cold front?

   _____   _____

   _____

5. The high temperature in Miami is expected to be 89°. What is the low temperature expected to be?

   _____

6. The low temperature in Dallas will be 72°. What will the high temperature be?

   _____

7. Which city will have a higher temperature—Seattle or Denver? _____

8. What state do you live in? According to this map, is it raining in your state? _____

Check your answers on page 193.

Exercise 2

Where do you think more people choose to live—in the mountains or along the seacoast?

Use the map and the background notes to complete the exercise.

Where People Live

Background notes: Population density is the average number of people living in an area. Many things can affect where people choose to live. One factor is the physical features of an area. For example, fewer people live in the mountains than along the seacoast because it is difficult to live in the mountains. Therefore, mountain areas have low population density, and coastal areas have high population density. It is also difficult to live in deserts and rain forests. These areas have low population density too.

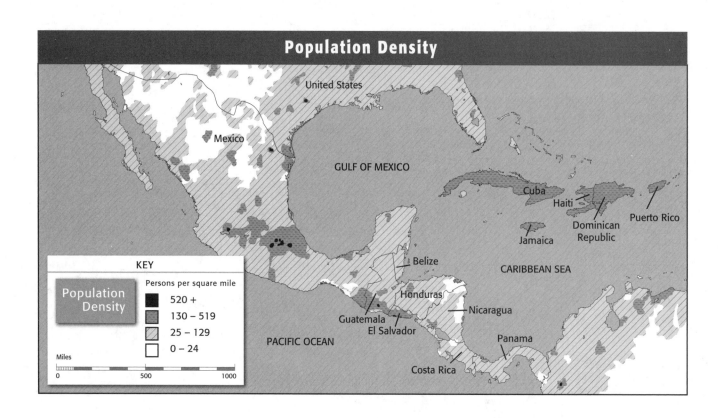

Population Density

KEY

Population Density

Persons per square mile

- 520 +
- 130 – 519
- 25 – 129
- 0 – 24

Miles

0   500   1000

1. Where do most people in Mexico live?
   (1) in the north
   (2) in central Mexico
   (3) in the south
   (4) in the southeast

2. What this the most logical reason that the island nations of Jamaica and Haiti have a high population density?
   (1) They are close to Cuba.
   (2) They are small.
   (3) The climate is pleasant.
   (4) Many tourists visit there.

3. Which nation does *not* have any areas of very high population density?
   (1) Mexico
   (2) Guatemala
   (3) Cuba
   (4) Panama

4. Most of the area in Honduras and Nicaragua has a population density of
   (1) 520+ persons per square mile
   (2) 130–519 persons per square mile
   (3) 25–129 persons per square mile
   (4) 0–24 persons per square mile

5. There are mountains in northern Mexico, and that area receives little rain. As a result, much of northern Mexico has a population density of
   (1) 520+ persons per square mile
   (2) 130–519 persons per square mile
   (3) 25–129 persons per square mile
   (4) 0–24 persons per square mile

6. Belize is mostly rain forest. As a result, that nation's highest population density is
   (1) 520+ persons per square mile
   (2) 130–519 persons per square mile
   (3) 25–129 persons per square mile
   (4) 0–24 persons per square mile

Check your answers on pages 193–194.

Exercise 3

Why do people from the same background choose to live together? Where do Native Americans live?

Use the map and the background notes to answer the questions.

LANGUAGE Tip

In the past, the people who lived in America before the Europeans arrived were called "Indians." Today these people are more often called "Native Americans."

Native American Lands

Background notes: An Indian reservation is public land set aside for Native Americans. One-third of all Native Americans live on reservations. Some reservations in the United States are supported by the federal government. Others are supported by state governments. Many Native Americans choose not to live on reservations.

Areas in the United States
Where Groups of Native Americans Live

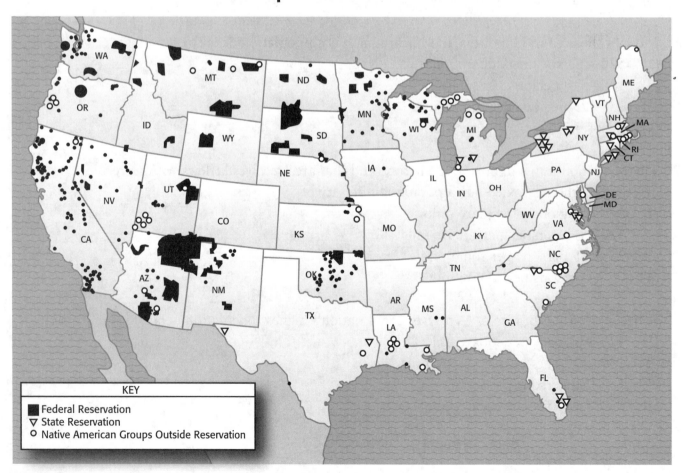

KEY
- ■ Federal Reservation
- ▽ State Reservation
- ○ Native American Groups Outside Reservation

1. Which of these states has the most land set aside for federal Native American reservations?
   - **(1)** Arizona
   - **(2)** New Mexico
   - **(3)** South Dakota
   - **(4)** North Dakota

2. Which of the following states has the fewest number of Native American groups living outside the reservations?
   - **(1)** Oregon
   - **(2)** Louisiana
   - **(3)** North Carolina
   - **(4)** Utah

3. Where is the greatest number of state reservations located?
   - **(1)** Florida
   - **(2)** South Carolina
   - **(3)** New York
   - **(4)** Maine

Check your answers on page 194.

Writing Workshop

Prewriting
In this chapter, you studied the symbols on a weather map. Using a weather map from your local newspaper (or the map on page 114), write notes describing the weather in several parts of the United States. Look for comparisons and contrasts.

Drafting
Pretend you are a weather reporter on a news program. Write a paragraph summarizing the weather conditions shown on the map. Tell people across the country what kind of weather they can expect.

Revising
Look for words that could be more specific. Instead of "north," would "northwest" be more accurate? Do you mean "rain," "sprinkles," or "storm"?

Editing
A small circle is used to represent "degrees." If you are using a computer, you can make this symbol by going to the **Insert** menu. Click **Symbol**. Then find and click the small circle. Click **Insert** to place the symbol in your paragraph.

Chapter 14

Finding Directions and Distances

Have you ever gotten lost by driving in the wrong direction? Do you always know how far you have to drive before you will reach your destination? Reading maps can help you figure out both directions and distances.

Routes to O'Hare International Airport

This map of the Chicago area shows where O'Hare International Airport is located. Study the map carefully. The numbers on the map refer to highways.

Northwestern Chicago, Illinois

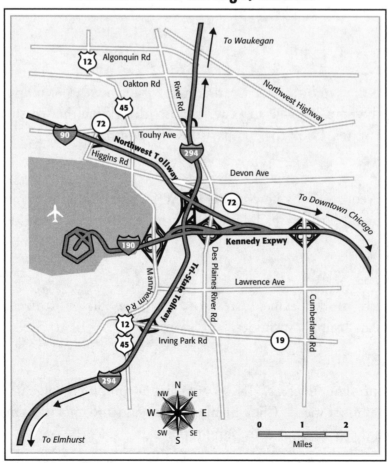

The **compass rose** on the bottom of the map marks the directions north, south, east, and west. Notice that directions such as northeast (NE) and southwest (SW) are also marked on this compass rose.

Real distances, such as miles, are represented on maps by much smaller lengths. The **scale** on the map is a drawing that looks like a small ruler. The mileage scale on this map is shown at the bottom of the map.

The scale helps you measure distances on a map. Mark off the distance between two places on the edge of a piece of paper. Then line up your paper next to the scale. The marks will help you estimate the distance between two places.

◆ **Suppose you want to drive to O'Hare International Airport. What direction would you travel in if you were leaving from each of these places?**

(1) Downtown Chicago _____   (3) Elmhurst _____

(2) Waukegan _____

Here are the correct answers: **northwest; southwest;** and **northeast.**

◆ **Next, try using the map's scale to estimate a distance. You are driving on Touhy Avenue. (This road is north of the airport.) Then you turn onto River Road. About how many miles would you travel before reaching Irving Park Road?**_____

You correctly estimated the distance if you wrote **about 5 miles.**

Strategy: **How to Find Directions and Distances**

- Find the compass rose on the map. North is usually at the top of the map.
- Find the distance represented in the map scale.
- Estimate the distance between two places by marking the distance on a piece of paper and comparing your marks to the map scale.

Exercise 1

What would your life be like if you had to keep moving to support your family? Where do some people go to find work in the United States?

Use the map and the background notes to answer the questions.

LANGUAGE Tip

No one knows for sure how many migrant workers are in the United States. A good estimate is about 3 million. Housing, health care, and education for children are problems for migrant workers.

Main Routes of Migrant Workers

Background notes: Migrant workers are people who often move, or migrate. Migrant workers harvest crops. They often move several times every year so they are ready to pick the crops that are ripe. Many of these workers come from Mexico. They find work in almost every state. This map shows the routes migrant workers take when they move to different farm areas.

Routes of Migrant Workers in the United States

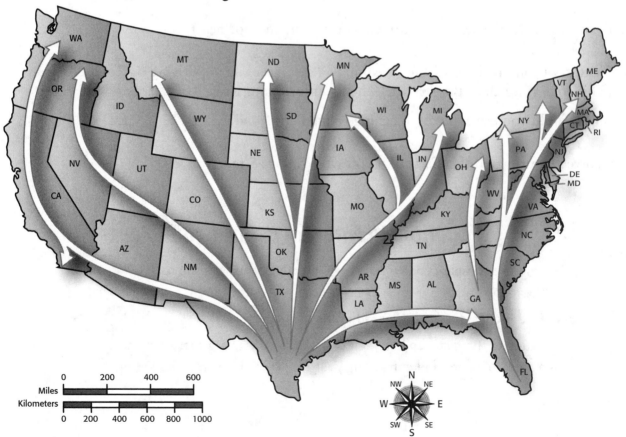

1. In which state do most of the main routes start? _____

2. In what general direction do most migrant workers travel? _____

3. About how many miles is the route beginning in Florida and ending in New York?

   _____

4. About how many miles is the route beginning in Georgia and ending in Ohio?

   _____

5. Which northeastern states are not touched by a migrant route?

   _____   _____   _____

6. About how many miles is the route beginning in Texas and ending in Oregon?

   _____

7. Which state is the beginning point for the route that ends in New York?

   _____

8. In which five states do migrant routes branch off into two paths?

   _____   _____   _____

   _____   _____

Check your answers on page 194.

Have you ever been in a heavy rainstorm that lasted for several hours? What do you think it would be like to live in a place where it rained for weeks at a time?

Use the map and the background notes to complete the exercises.

The Monsoons in India

Background notes: Monsoons are seasonal winds. Every year the monsoons bring heavy rain to India, Bangladesh, and other parts of south Asia. The monsoon season lasts from June to September. Parts of western and central India receive about 90 percent of their yearly rainfall during these months. Areas in southern and northwestern India receive 50 to 70 percent of their yearly rainfall during these months. Some parts of India receive as much as 100 inches of rain during the monsoon season. Then the winds shift. From September to March, they blow hot, dry air over India and Bangladesh.

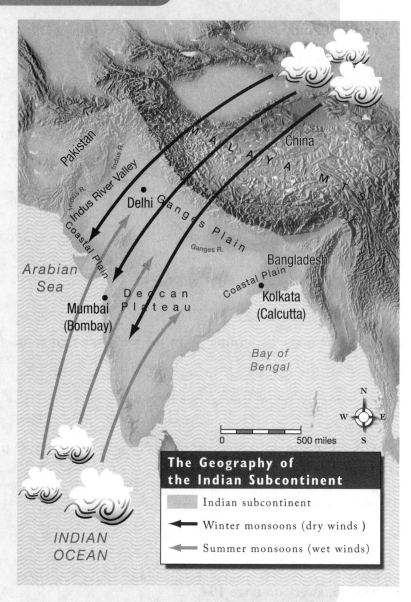

The Geography of the Indian Subcontinent

- Indian subcontinent
- → Winter monsoons (dry winds)
- → Summer monsoons (wet winds)

1. In what direction do the monsoon winds blow from June to September?
   (1) north
   (2) northeast
   (3) south
   (4) southwest

2. In what direction do the monsoon winds blow from September to March?
   (1) north
   (2) northeast
   (3) south
   (4) southwest

3. What direction is China from India?
   (1) south
   (2) west
   (3) northeast
   (4) northwest

4. If the monsoons were to drop heavy rain on Pakistan, which direction would they need to blow farther in?
   (1) north
   (2) south
   (3) east
   (4) west

5. The Bay of Bengal is about _____ at its widest point.

6. The distance between Mumbai and Kolkata is about _____.

7. The distance from Delhi to Mumbai is about _____.

Check your answers on page 194.

Exercise 3

Why did some people take a bus trip called "The Freedom Ride"? What was the purpose of their journey?

Use the map and the background notes to answer the questions.

The Freedom Ride

Background notes: In 1961, the Congress of Racial Equality (CORE) organized the "Freedom Ride." The goal of this long bus trip was to put pressure on the U.S. government so the government would protect the civil rights of African Americans. The Supreme Court had decided in 1946 that segregation on buses traveling between states was illegal. However, the government was not enforcing this law. People on the Freedom Ride risked their lives for civil rights.

Both African Americans and whites took part in the Freedom Ride. The plan was for African Americans to sit in the front of the bus. If ordered to move to the back of the bus, they would refuse.

The Freedom Ride began in Washington, D.C., on May 4. It ended in the state of Louisiana. Riders met with violence all along the way. Some people were badly beaten. Others spent time in jail. The Freedom Ride was an important step toward civil rights for African Americans.

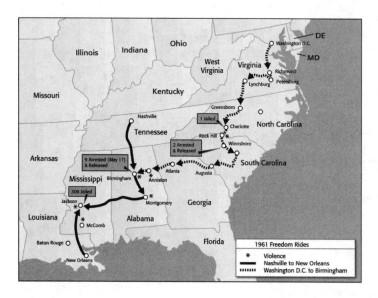

1. From Washington, D.C., the Freedom Ride headed _____ and then _____.

2. From Montgomery, the Freedom Ride traveled _____ and then _____.

3. The Freedom Ride traveled through the states of _____, _____, _____, _____, _____, _____, _____, and _____.

4. The distance traveled from Montgomery to Jackson was about _____.

5. The distance traveled from Jackson to New Orleans was about _____.

6. The total distance covered from Montgomery to New Orleans was about _____.

7. The distance from Nashville to Montgomery is about _____.

Check your answers on page 194.

Writing Workshop

Prewriting
You have read about the travels of migrant workers and Freedom Riders. Think about a trip you have made. List details such as where you went, what you saw along the way, who was with you, and why you were traveling. Organize the details into categories.

Drafting
Use your list to write an entry in a diary, or journal. Make up dates and describe what happened on each of those dates.

Revising
Most people write in diaries the way they talk. Shorten your sentences. Use exclamation points when you have something exciting to tell about.

Editing
Check that contractions are spelled correctly. The apostrophe should be placed where letters have been omitted. Examples: I'm (I am), we'll (we will), can't (cannot).

Historical Maps

Historical maps help you learn about the past. They can show you what an area looked like many years ago. Historical maps may explain events, trends, or political ideas.

For example, the following map can help you understand the history of immigrants in the United States. Immigrants are people who move from one country to another. Between 1820 and 1920, almost 30 million immigrants came to the United States. Study the map carefully. Find where various immigrant groups first settled.

Early Settlers: 1820–1920

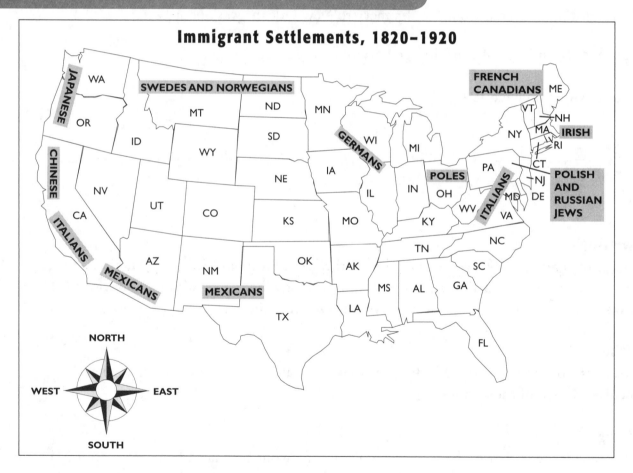

Immigrant Settlements, 1820–1920

◆ Use the map to answer the questions.

1. Which immigrant group first settled in both the east and the west? _____

2. In which four states did Mexicans first settle?

_____ _____ _____ _____

LANGUAGE Tip

Prefixes

The prefix *im-* means "in" or "into." The prefix *e-* means "from."

   Carlos **immigrated to** the United States.

   Carlos **emigrated from** Mexico.

3. Which immigrant group first settled in Ohio (OH)?

   _____

4. Which two immigrant groups first settled near the northern border of the United States?

   _____   _____

5. In which state did French Canadians first settle?

   _____

6. Which immigrant group first settled in Massachusetts (MA)? _____

7. In which three states did Chinese and Japanese immigrants first settle?

   _____   _____   _____

8. In which four states did Germans first settle?

   _____   _____   _____   _____

9. On what coast did Polish and Russian Jews first settle? _____

Here are the correct answers:

1. Italians

2. Arizona (AZ), California (CA), New Mexico (NM), and Texas (TX)

3. Poles

4. Swedes and Norwegians; French Canadians.

5. Maine (ME)

6. Irish

7. California (CA), Oregon (OR), and Washington (WA)

8. Illinois (IL), Iowa (IA), Minnesota (MN), and Wisconsin (WI)

9. east

Strategy: **How to Understand Historical Maps**

- Read the title and background information.
- If the map has a key, locate the symbols on the map.
- Think about the events, trends, or ideas that are shown on the map.

Exercise 1

What would you do if you were denied the right to vote? What steps did women take to gain this right?

Use the map and the background notes to answer the questions.

Women's Voting Rights: 1914

Background notes: *Suffrage* means "the right to vote." In 1869, the National Women's Suffrage Association was formed. Two women, Elizabeth Cady Stanton and Susan B. Anthony, headed this group. Their goal was to add an amendment to the Constitution that would give women the right to vote. On March 3, 1913, thousands of women staged a protest. They marched in Washington, D.C., to support suffrage. This map shows information about women's suffrage in 1914. (The photograph on page 110 shows a 1916 parade in New York City to support women's right to vote.)

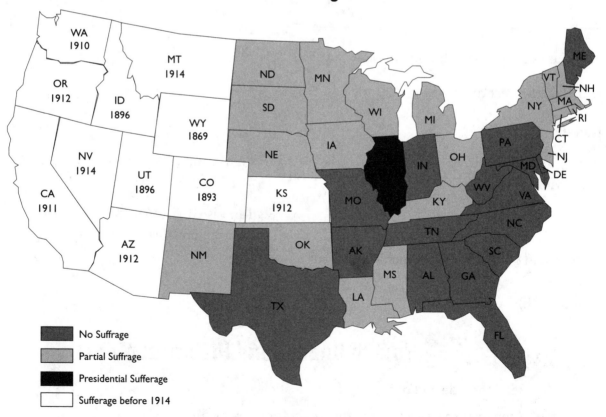

Women's Suffrage, 1914

1. What is the subject, or topic, of this map?

   _____

2. What was the goal of the National Women's Suffrage Association?

   _____

   _____

3. (a) By 1914, which 11 states had given women the right to vote?

   _____   _____   _____

   _____   _____   _____

   _____   _____   _____

   _____   _____

   (b) Where are most of these states located—in the east, west, north, or south?

   _____

4. In which state could a woman vote only for president?

   _____

5. List at least six states that still denied women the right to vote in 1914.

   _____   _____

   _____   _____

   _____   _____

Check your answers on page 194.

Exercise 2

By the late 1800s, most of Africa was controlled by European countries. However, two African nations remained independent. What were these countries?

Read the passage and answer each question.

Colonies on the African Continent

Background notes: Europeans had traveled to the African continent for centuries. Portugal was the first modern European nation to set up a colony in Africa. It took control of Mozambique in 1500. Other European nations began to colonize Africa in the 1800s. By the 1880s, most of Africa had been divided up into European colonies.

Colonies in Africa, 1914

☐ Independent
☐ British Colonies
☐ French Colonies
☐ Other Colonies

0   500   1000 miles

1. How many colonies were governed by the British? _____

2. Which three European nations divided up and governed the East African country of Somaliland?

   _____ _____ _____

3. Which colony was directly south of German Southwest Africa? _____

4. Which two nations remained independent?

   _____ _____

5. Which nation governed the island of Madagascar? _____

6. About how far is it from Cairo, Egypt, to Johannesburg, South Africa? _____

7. Which two colonies were directly west of Anglo-Egyptian Sudan?

   _____

   _____

8. In what part of Africa was the Italian colony of Libya? _____

Check your answers on page 194.

Exercise 3

Did you know that some major California cities were once missions started by the Spanish?

Use the map and the background notes to answer the questions.

California Missions: 1769–1848

Background notes: In 1769, California was under Spanish rule. The Spanish government established many missions along the West Coast. These missions were settlements run by the Catholic Church. It took about a day to walk from one mission to the next. In 1822, California was brought under Mexican rule.

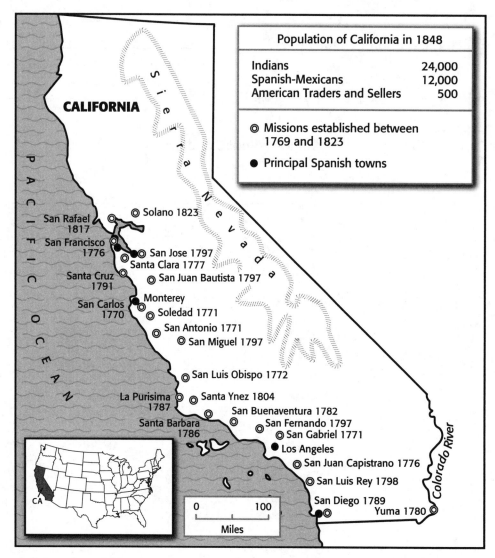

Population of California in 1848

Indians	24,000
Spanish-Mexicans	12,000
American Traders and Sellers	500

◎ Missions established between 1769 and 1823

● Principal Spanish towns

CALIFORNIA

Sierra Nevada

PACIFIC OCEAN

San Rafael 1817
San Francisco 1776
Solano 1823
San Jose 1797
Santa Clara 1777
Santa Cruz 1791
San Juan Bautista 1797
Monterey
San Carlos 1770
Soledad 1771
San Antonio 1771
San Miguel 1797
San Luis Obispo 1772
La Purisima 1787
Santa Ynez 1804
San Buenaventura 1782
Santa Barbara 1786
San Fernando 1797
San Gabriel 1771
Los Angeles
San Juan Capistrano 1776
San Luis Rey 1798
San Diego 1789
Yuma 1780
Colorado River

CA

0   100
Miles

1. How many missions were established before 1800? _____

2. How many missions were founded after 1800? _____

3. Which town is located directly north of San Carlos? _____

4. Name two missions that became big California cities.

    _____

    _____

5. What is the approximate distance between San Diego and Santa Barbara? _____

6. What is the approximate distance between San Francisco and Monterey? _____

Check your answers on page 194.

 # Writing Workshop

Prewriting
In this chapter, you studied a map that gave information about immigrants. What country did your ancestors come from? When did they arrive? Where did they settle? Where are they now? Write the answers to these questions.

Drafting
Organize your answers into a paragraph. Your main-idea sentence should explain your family's history. Each detail should tell about your family's roots.

Revising
Check that details about each family member are grouped together. If you write about several family members, you might use a new paragraph for each person.

Editing
Be sure that words made from the name of a place are capitalized. Examples: Cuban, Polish, Japanese, Texan, Californian.

Review – Geography

What was the relationship between railroad lines and cattle trails in the late 1800s?

Use the map and the background notes to answer the questions.

Moving People and Cattle

Background notes: Cattle ranchers, cowboys, farmers, and railroad workers helped settle the West. Railroads made life easier for cattle ranchers. Cowboys drove herds of cattle to railroad towns. The railroads then shipped the cattle to large cities.

Railroads and Cattle Trails

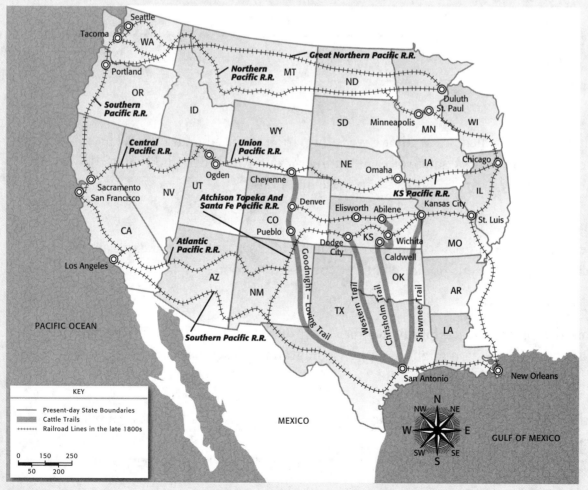

KEY

— Present-day State Boundaries
■ Cattle Trails
++++ Railroad Lines in the late 1800s

0   150   250
  50   200

1. What is the name of the longest cattle trail?
   (1) Shawnee Trail
   (2) Chisholm Trail
   (3) Western Trail
   (4) Goodnight-Loving Trail

2. Which railroad traveled north up the California coast?
   (1) Southern Pacific
   (2) Central Pacific
   (3) Atlantic and Pacific
   (4) Northern Pacific

3. How many miles is it from San Antonio to Caldwell on the Chisholm Trail?
   (1) about 350 miles
   (2) about 400 miles
   (3) about 450 miles
   (4) about 500 miles

4. Which of the following cities was connected to three railroad lines?
   (1) New Orleans, Louisiana
   (2) Chicago, Illinois
   (3) Dodge City, Kansas
   (4) Abilene, Kansas

5. Which of the following was connected to four cattle trails?
   (1) New Orleans, Louisiana
   (2) Kansas City, Missouri
   (3) San Antonio, Texas
   (4) Pueblo, Colorado

6. Which cattle trail ended in Kansas City?
   (1) Shawnee Trail
   (2) Chisholm Trail
   (3) Western Trail
   (4) Goodnight-Loving Trail

Check your answers on page 195.

UNIT 5

Economics

WHAT PRODUCTS AND services do people buy? How do people earn and spend their money? How do businesses and governments manage money? **Economics** is the branch of social sciences that addresses these questions.

Information about economics is often presented in charts and graphs. By reading charts and graphs, you can learn important facts and figures.

Chapter	What You Will Learn About	What You Will Read
16	Charts	Why People Like Their Jobs Job Characteristics Economic Data Salaries of Professional Athletes
17	Line Graphs	The Great Depression Women in the Workforce Oil Producers Government Budgets
18	Bar Graphs	Music Sales Injuries on the Job U.S. Trade Partners How Much Will I Earn?
19	Circle Graphs	A Family Budget Child Support Payments Foreign Aid The Cost of Being an Employer
Review	Economics	Education

After reading this unit, you should understand

- charts
- line graphs
- bar graphs
- circle graphs

Chapter 16

Charts

Charts summarize useful information. Train schedules are charts that tell you about times, fares, and places. The sports sections of newspapers are filled with charts about teams and players.

Charts are often used in economics to make facts clear to the reader. The title of a chart tells you what the chart is about. The numbers and words in a chart are organized into columns and rows.

Practice your skill in reading a chart by answering these questions about workers who are happy with their jobs.

Why People Like Their Jobs

Workers Who Are Happy with Their Jobs		Workers Who Are Unhappy with Their Jobs	
Occupation	% Very Happy	Occupation	% Very Happy
Pastors, Priests, Rabbis	87%	Clothing Salespersons	24%
Firefighters	80%	Food Preparers	24%
Physical Therapists	78%	Cashiers	25%
Teachers	69%	Bartenders	26%
Office Supervisors	61%	Waiters, Servers	27%

Source: General Social Survey, University of Chicago, 2006

1. What does the chart compare and contrast?

   _____

2. Which workers are the happiest with their jobs? _____

3. In which occupations are at least three-fourths (75%) of workers happy with their jobs?

_____

4. How are the top three occupations alike? _____

5. Which workers are the least happy with their jobs? _____

6. How are the jobs of the most unhappy workers alike? _____

7. What can you infer about the education of people who are happy with their jobs?

_____

Here are the answers:

1. The chart compares and contrasts jobs that usually make people happy with jobs that often do not make people happy.
2. pastors, priests, and rabbis
3. pastors, priests, and rabbis; firefighters; physical therapists
4. These workers help people.
5. clothing salespersons and food preparers
6. These workers have jobs in customer service. Most of them are in food service.
7. These people have all had special training for their jobs. In contrast, people who are unhappy with their jobs are doing jobs that require little training.

Strategy: How to Read a Chart

- Read the title. What is the topic of the chart?
- Read the headings for the columns and the rows. What kind of information is presented on the chart?
- Study all the facts and figures.
- Notice how the facts and figures are related. Look for comparisons and contrasts.

Exercise 1

How is your job like the jobs of other U.S. workers? How is it different?

Study the chart and complete the exercise.

LANGUAGE Tip

A worker who earns **wages** is paid by the hour. A worker who earns a **salary** is paid a set amount per year.

Job Characteristics

How Workers Describe Their Jobs	Percent of Workers Who Agree
Worked at present job 2 years or less	39%
Receive an annual salary	34%
Paid by the hour	53%
Work a day shift	70%
Work an irregular schedule	10%
Have more than one job	17%
Need to learn new things on the job	85%
Are proud to work for current employer	88%
Feel a need for a strong labor union	45%
Work as a team member	57%
Have good chances for a promotion	54%
Have good benefits (vacations, etc.)	78%
Are likely to get bonuses for good work	24%
Feel salary or wages are fair	56%
Have flexible hours if needed	54%
Have 3 or more close friends at work	36%

Source: *American Attitudes,* 2005

Read each statement. Circle *T* if it is true or *F* if it is false.

T F 1. Most workers want unions to help them get better pay.

T F 2. Most workers are happy with their vacations, pensions, and holidays.

T F 3. Half of all workers have night shifts.

T F 4. About half of all workers think they are paid fairly.

T F 5. Nearly all workers are proud of the companies they work for.

T F 6. Only a few workers have more than one job.

T F 7. Most employers will not let their workers go to a doctor's appointment during the day.

T F 8. About half of all U.S. workers are paid by the hour.

T F 9. Workers usually have many close friends at their jobs.

T F 10. From the chart, you can infer that most workers expect to stay at their current job for a long time.

T F 11. Nearly all U.S. workers work in teams.

T F 12. Nearly all workers must learn on the job.

Check your answers on page 195.

Exercise 2

Economic information can help us understand a nation. For example, how does poverty affect a nation?

Study the chart and complete the exercise.

LANGUAGE *Tip*

The **gross domestic product (GDP)** is the value of all the goods and services produced in a country in one year. In 2005, the GDP in the United States was $41,800 per person.

Economic Data

Data from Five Latin American Countries in a Recent Year

	Brazil	Costa Rica	Mexico	Panama	Peru
Population	190 million	4 million	108 million	3 million	28 million
Labor force	97.8 million	1.8 million	44.5 million	1.4 million	9.2 million
GDP (in $ per person)	$8,800	$12,500	$10,700	$8,200	$6,600
Unemployment Rate	9.6%	6.6%	3.2%	8.8%	7.2%
% of Population Below Poverty Line	31%	18%	18%	37%	53%
Value of Exports	$137.8 billion	$8.2 billion	$250 billion	$8.5 billion	$23.7 billion
Value of Imports	$91.4 billion	$10.8 billion	$256.1 billion	$10.3 billion	$14.9 billion
Top 5 Farm Products	coffee, soybeans, wheat, rice, corn	bananas, pineapples, coffee, melons, plants	corn, wheat, soybeans, rice, beans	bananas, rice, corn, coffee, sugarcane	asparagus, coffee, cotton, sugarcane, rice
Top 5 Industries	textiles, shoes, chemicals, cement, lumber	electronics, food, textiles and clothing, building materials, fertilizer	food and beverages, tobacco, chemicals, iron and steel, oil	construction, brewing, cement, building materials, sugar milling	mining, steel, oil, natural gas, fishing

Source: *The World Factbook,* Central Intelligence Agency, U.S. Government

1. Which nation listed on the chart has the largest population? _____

2. In which nation do more than half of the people live below the poverty line? _____

3. Which nations grow rice? _____

4. In which nation is electronics an important industry? _____

5. Cotton is an important farm product in which nation? _____

6. Which nation has the highest GDP? _____

7. Which nation has the lowest GDP? _____

8. Which nation has the lowest unemployment rate? _____

9. Is Panama's unemployment rate higher or lower than Brazil's unemployment rate? _____

10. Which two nations export more goods than they import?

_____

11. Does the nation with the lowest unemployment rate also have the fewest people living below the poverty line? _____

12. The "labor force" is the number of possible workers. In which country is more than half of the population in the labor force? _____

Check your answers on page 195.

How much money do professional athletes earn? These charts provide information about some professional athletes. Do you think the players are worth so much money?

Study the two charts and answer the questions.

Salaries of Professional Athletes

REPORTED SALARIES IN THE NBA			
Player	**Team**	**Joined NBA**	**2007 Salary**
Kevin Garnett	Minnesota	1995	$21,000,000
Shaquille O'Neal	Miami	1992	$20,000,000
Jason Kidd	New Jersey	1994	$18,084,000
Allen Iverson	Denver	1996	$17,184, 375
Stephon Marbury	New York	1996	$17,184,375

REPORTED SALARIES IN MAJOR LEAGUE BASEBALL			
Player	**Team**	**Joined Majors**	**2007 Salary**
Alex Rodriguez	New York Yankees	1995	$27,708,525
Jason Giambi	New York Yankees	1996	$23,428,571
Derek Jeter	New York Yankees	1996	$21,600,000
Manny Ramirez	Boston Red Sox	1994	$17,016,381
Todd Helton	Colorado Rockies	1998	$16,600,000

1. What was Shaquille O'Neill's 2007 salary? _____

2. Among top-paid NBA players, who had played professional basketball the longest,

   as of 2007? _____

3. Which two basketball players earned the same salary in 2007?

   _____ _____

4. Which two basketball players had played in the NBA the fewest years, as of 2007?

   _____ _____

5. Which NBA player earned the highest salary in 2007? _____

6. How much money did Derek Jeter earn in 2007? _____

7. In 2007, which baseball team had the most players with high salaries? _____

8. Which of the highest-paid baseball players had played the fewest years in Major League Baseball, as of 2007? _____

9. In 2007, which baseball players earned more than the highest-paid NBA player?

_____

10. Which of the highest-paid baseball players joined Major League Baseball the same year that Kevin Garnett began playing in the NBA?

_____

Check your answers on page 195.

 # Writing Workshop

Prewriting
Some people think that professional athletes make too much money. Write a list of reasons why you agree or disagree with this opinion.

Drafting
Write a letter to the editor about professional athletes' salaries. State your opinion in one sentence. Then give reasons for your opinion. Include facts to support your opinion.

Revising
In your letter, have you recognized that there is more than one opinion about this topic? By doing so, you show that you are open to thinking about all sides of a problem.

Editing
Be sure that words showing possession are correctly spelled.

For singular names, add an apostrophe and an *s*.   Thomas's bat
For plural names ending in *s*, add an apostrophe.   the Yankees' score
For plural names not ending in *s*, add an apostrophe and an *s*.   men's shirts

Chapter 17

Line Graphs

Line graphs can help you understand the facts and figures used in economics. The **line on the graph** shows a change over time. The line connects points on the graph. By studying how the line moves, you can figure out trends, or general movements.

Look at the graph below. The title tells you the topic and the time period of the information on the graph. The label on the bottom of the graph shows the years. Each mark represents one year. The label on the side represents the percentage (%) of people who were unemployed in the United States. A line slanting upward shows an increase in unemployed people. A line slanting downward shows a decrease.

The Great Depression

Background notes: The Great Depression began in 1929 when the banks failed and most people lost their savings. It ended in 1939, about the time World War II began. During the war, almost no one was unemployed.

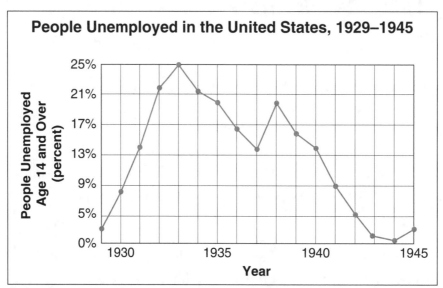

Source: *Historical Statistics of the United States, Colonial Times to 1970*

Read the title and the labels before you answer these questions.

How would you find the percentage of people without jobs in 1933? Put your finger on the year 1933 on the bottom of the graph. Move your finger straight up until you reach the dot. Notice that you have reached the highest point marked on the graph. Next, read across to the number on the left side of the graph.

What percentage of people were unemployed in 1933? _____

The correct answer is **25%**.

◆ **Practice your skill in reading line graphs. Answer the following questions.**

1. After what year did the number of unemployed people begin to decrease? _____

2. What percentage of people were unemployed in 1944? _____

3. What percentage of people were unemployed in 1930? _____

4. In what year was the percentage of unemployed people 5%? _____

5. What percentage of people were unemployed in 1937? _____

6. In what year was there almost full employment? _____

Here are the correct answers:

1. 1933   2. about 1%   3. 8%   4. 1942   5. 14%   6. 1944

By reading this graph, you have learned some important facts and figures about the economic history of the United States. During the 1930s, the poor economy meant that many people were unemployed.

Strategy: How to Read a Line Graph

- Read the title. What is the topic of the graph?
- Read the labels on the bottom and the side of the graph to see what the numbers represent.
- Study the shape of the line. What changes do you notice? Does the line show an increase, a decrease, or both?
- Locate points by reading the numbers on both the bottom and the side of the graph.
- Think about the relationship between the numbers on the graph.

Exercise 1

Why are more women working? How does the economy benefit from working women?

Study the line graph and answer the questions.

Women in the Workforce

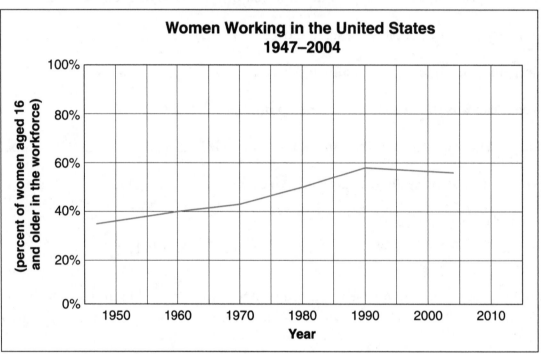

Women Working in the United States 1947–2004

Source: Bureau of Labor Statistics

PART A

1. What period of time is covered in the graph? _____

2. What do the numbers on the side of the graph represent? _____

3. What trend does the graph show?

_____

_____

4. What percentage of women worked in 1960? _____

5. In what year did about 60% of women hold jobs? _____

6. During what 20-year period did the fastest growth of women in the workforce occur?

_____

7. What is the approximate change in percentage of women working from 1947 to 2004?

_____

PART B

1. In what year were about half of all women working?
   (1) 1965
   (2) 1980
   (3) 1985
   (4) 1990

2. By about what percent did the number of working women increase from 1980 to 2000?
   (1) 40%
   (2) 30%
   (3) 20%
   (4) 10%

3. In what year did about 45% of women hold jobs?
   (1) 1955
   (2) 1960
   (3) 1975
   (4) 2000

Check your answers on page 196.

Exercise 2

Iran, Iraq, and Venezuela are three of the top ten oil producers in the world. Together these three nations produce about 10 percent of the world's oil. What do you know about these nations?

Study the line graph. Then answer the questions.

LANGUAGE Tip

The word *produce* can be a noun or a verb. The noun and the verb are pronounced in different ways.

PROH doos   things that are
(noun)   made or grown

proh DOOS   to make
(verb)

Oil Producers

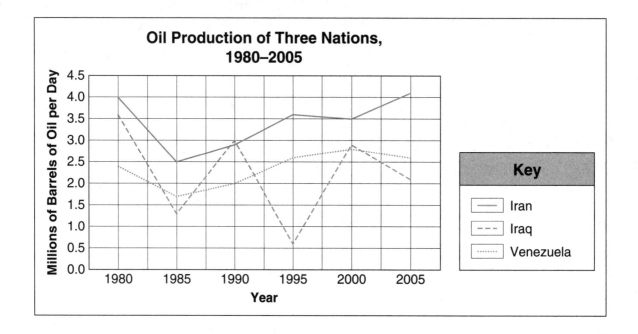

1. In which year did Iran and Iraq produce about the same amount of oil per day?
   (1) 1985
   (2) 1990
   (3) 1995
   (4) 2000

2. After which year did Iraq's oil production begin its greatest decline?
   (1) 1980
   (2) 1985
   (3) 1990
   (4) 1995

3. About how many barrels of oil per day did Iran produce in 2005?
   (1) 1 million
   (2) 2.5 million
   (3) 3.5 million
   (4) 4 million

4. What does the graph show about oil production between 1990 and 1995 for all three nations?
   (1) Oil production changed very little in the three nations.
   (2) All three nations produced more oil in 1995 than in 1990.
   (3) All three nations produced less oil in 1995 than in 1990.
   (4) Oil production changed a great deal in all three nations.

5. In which year did Venezuela produce the most oil per day?
   (1) 1980
   (2) 1990
   (3) 2000
   (4) 2005

6. Which statement most accurately describes Iraq's oil production over the 25 years shown on the graph?
   (1) Oil production has varied greatly.
   (2) Oil production has been generally increasing.
   (3) Oil production has been generally decreasing.
   (4) The number of barrels produced per day has remained steady.

Check your answers on page 196.

Exercise 3

How does the government spend money? Does the government spend more money than it receives?

Study the line graph. Then answer the questions.

LANGUAGE Tip

Governments and businesses often write their budgets for the **fiscal year**. Instead of beginning their budget year on January 1, they may begin it on April 1 or July 1.

Government Budgets

Source: Office of Management and Budget

1. During which year did the government spend almost exactly as much money as it received?
   - **(1)** 1943
   - **(2)** 1970
   - **(3)** 1985
   - **(4)** 2000

2. In what year did government spending decrease by the largest amount?
   - **(1)** 1946
   - **(2)** 1965
   - **(3)** 1980
   - **(4)** 2000

3. During which years did the government receive more money than it spent?
   - **(1)** 1940–1945
   - **(2)** 1955–1965
   - **(3)** 1983–1985
   - **(4)** 1999–2001

4. What does the graph show about spending in the 1960s?
   (1) The government spent much more money than it received.
   (2) The government collected much more tax money than it spent.
   (3) Spending and income were about equal.
   (4) The government began to spend less money than it had in previous years.

5. From the information on the graph, what can you infer about government spending and income after 2008?
   (1) The government will have to spend less or tax more.
   (2) The government will always spend more money than it receives.
   (3) The government will stop spending money.
   (4) The government will double taxes.

Check your answers on page 196.

Writing Workshop

Prewriting

In the early 1990s, many people lost their jobs. How do you think unemployed people feel? What money problems do they face? Write a list describing the effects of being unemployed. Choose one effect to write about.

Drafting

Write a topic sentence that states the main point you would like to discuss. Then develop your topic sentence into a paragraph. Add details that explain one effect of being unemployed.

Revising

Look for simple sentences that can be combined. Use a comma when you connect two simple sentences with *and, but,* or *or.*

> People look for new jobs, but good jobs are hard to find.

Editing

Check that your subjects and verbs agree.

| Singular | The **worker loses** his health insurance. |
| Plural | **Companies go** out of business. |

Bar Graphs

Most people enjoy listening to music. How much money do people spend on different types of music? The answer to this question can be shown on a bar graph.

A **bar graph** uses bars to show comparisons and contrasts. The title explains the topic. The labels on the bottom of the bar graph tell you what each bar represents. The label and the numbers on the side of the bar graph help you figure out the height of each bar.

Study this bar graph. Notice the difference in the height of the bars.

Music Sales

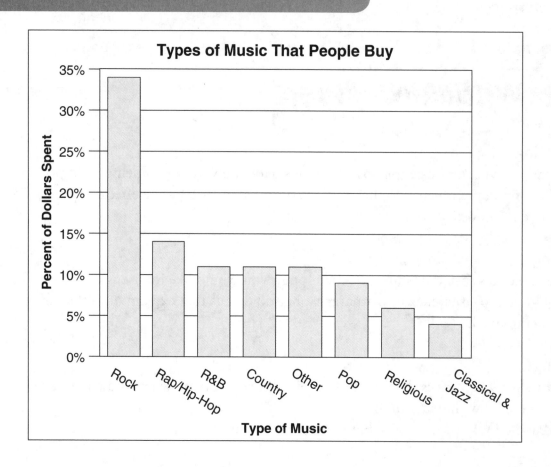

◆ Practice your skill in reading a bar graph. Answer these questions.

1. What type of music is bought the most? _____

2. What type of music is bought the least? _____

3. What type of music represents 9% of the music

    purchased? _____

LANGUAGE *Tip*

The bars on a bar graph can be vertical (up and down) or horizontal (left to right). Labels always tell you what the bars represent.

4. What percentage of music purchased is religious? _____

5. Which type of music do people buy more of—country or pop? _____

6. What type of music represents 14% of music purchased? _____

7. Which types of music sell about the same amount?

_____

Here are the correct answers:
1. rock
2. classical and jazz
3. pop
4. 6%

5. country
6. rap and hip-hop
7. R&B, country, and other

Strategy: **How to Read a Bar Graph**

- Read the title. What is the topic of the graph?
- Read the labels on the bottom of the graph. What does each bar represent?
- Read the labels on the side of the graph. What do the numbers represent?
- Compare and contrast the height or length of the bars.
- Notice changes, or trends, represented by the height of the bars.

Exercise 1

Why are employers concerned about safety on the job? How often do workers die from job injuries? How is the number of work-related deaths in the United States changing?

Study the bar graph and answer the questions.

LANGUAGE Tip

OSHA   **OH shah**

OSHA is the U.S. government's Occupational Safety and Health Administration. All accidents that happen while someone is working must be reported to OSHA.

Injuries on the Job

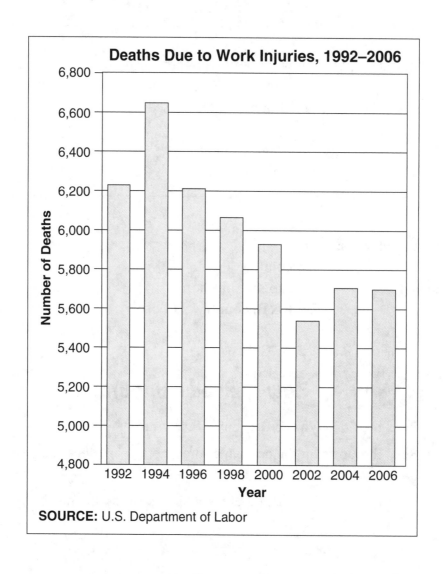

Deaths Due to Work Injuries, 1992–2006

SOURCE: U.S. Department of Labor

1. What is the topic of this graph? _____

2. What do the numbers on the left side of the bar graph represent?

   _____

3. About how many work-related deaths were there in 1994?

   _____

4. In which two years was the number of deaths almost the same?

   _____

5. Between which years did the number of deaths continually decrease?

   _____

6. In which year were there the fewest work-related deaths?

   _____

7. How many more deaths were there in 2004 than in 2002?

   _____

8. What can you infer, or figure out, is the most logical reason that the number of deaths on the job is usually decreasing?
   (1)   There are fewer workers each year.
   (2)   Fewer accidents are reported.
   (3)   Workers learn better safety skills.
   (4)   The government has not completed the report.

Check your answers on page 196.

Exercise 2

World trade is an important part of the nation's economy. What products do U.S. businesses sell to other countries? What products do U.S. businesses buy from other nations?

Read the passage. Then circle the best answer for each question.

U.S. Trade Partners

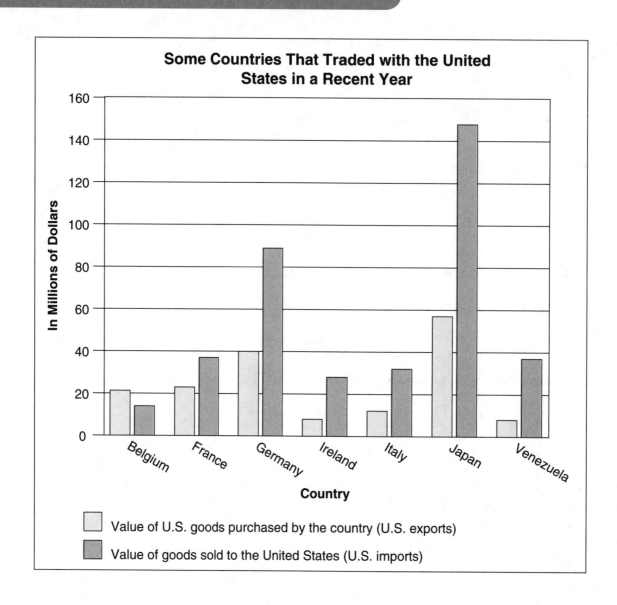

Some Countries That Traded with the United States in a Recent Year

In Millions of Dollars

Country

☐ Value of U.S. goods purchased by the country (U.S. exports)

■ Value of goods sold to the United States (U.S. imports)

1. From which of the nations listed on the graph did the United States buy the most goods?
   (1) France
   (2) Germany
   (3) Japan
   (4) Venezuela

2. Which nation had the smallest difference between what it sold to the United States and what it bought?
   (1) Belgium
   (2) Ireland
   (3) Italy
   (4) Venezuela

3. Which nation bought the most goods from the United States?
   (1) Germany
   (2) Ireland
   (3) Italy
   (4) Japan

4. What is the value of U.S. goods sold to France?
   (1) a little more than $20 million
   (2) about $30 million
   (3) about $40 million
   (4) less than $20 million

5. Which two nations bought the smallest amount of goods from the United States?
   (1) Belgium and Ireland
   (2) Ireland and Italy
   (3) Italy and Venezuela
   (4) Venezuela and Ireland

6. What comparison is shown in this bar graph?
   (1) the total value of U.S. exports and imports in a year
   (2) trade between nations in Europe and Asia
   (3) the difference between U.S. imports and exports to and from certain countries
   (4) the change in U.S. exports and imports over time

Check your answers on page 196.

Exercise 3

How much money do workers earn in various occupations? How much can workers expect their wages to increase from year to year?

Study the bar graph. Then circle the best answer for each question.

How Much Will I Earn?

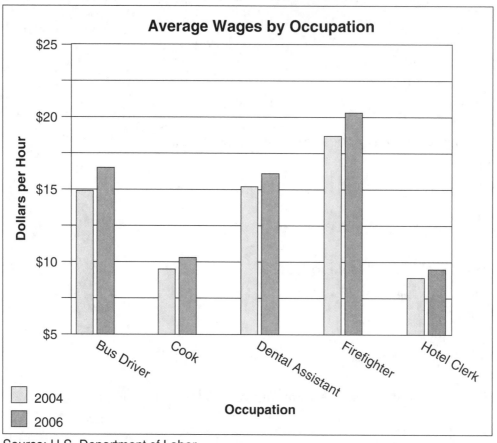

Source: U.S. Department of Labor

1. Which worker earned the highest wages in both 2004 and 2006?
   (1) hotel clerk
   (2) cook
   (3) firefighter
   (4) dental assistant

2. What does the graph show about the wages of various workers in 2006?
   (1) Bus drivers and firefighters earn almost the same wages.
   (2) Hotel clerks earn half as much as dental assistants.
   (3) The average cook earns less than the average hotel clerk.
   (4) A firefighter earns about twice as much as a cook.

3. Which workers had the greatest wage increase between 2004 and 2006?
   (1) bus driver and cook
   (2) cook and hotel clerk
   (3) dental assistant and firefighter
   (4) firefighter and bus driver

4. What can you infer, or figure out, from the graph?
   (1) More bus drivers are needed than cooks.
   (2) Wages usually increase a little each year.
   (3) Being a dental assistant is easier than being a bus driver.
   (4) Firefighters work more hours each week than other workers.

Check your answers on page 197.

Writing Workshop

Prewriting
Prepare a list of questions to ask about the job you would like to have. (Tip: Do not ask how much someone earns.) Interview a person who has that job. Listen carefully and take notes during your interview.

Drafting
Write a paragraph about this job. Use the answers to your questions for the details in your paragraph. Write a concluding sentence that explains why you would like this job.

Revising
Try to improve your job description by adding adverbs. Adverbs tell how something happens. Many adverbs end in *-ly*.

   As a nurse, Miriam works **quickly** but **carefully**.

Editing
If you are writing your paragraph on a computer, be sure to use the spell-check tool. However, you must remember that the computer will not find all the errors. For example, you must decide whether *their, there,* or *they're* is the correct word.

Chapter 19

Circle Graphs

How do you spend your money? What portion of your paycheck do you spend on rent or on food? A circle graph can help you see how your expenses break down.

A **circle graph** shows how parts relate to the whole. Each portion of the circle graph looks like a slice of a pie. Each "slice," or section, of a circle graph is a different size. The whole circle represents 100 percent. Each section of the circle represents a part of the whole amount. The sum of all the sections is 100 percent.

The circle graph below shows how the average American spends money. The labels name the expenses that most families have. Study the information shown on the circle graph. Then think about how you spend your money.

A Family Budget

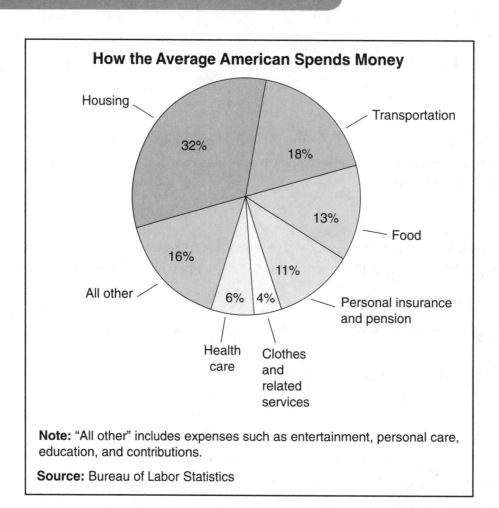

How the Average American Spends Money

- Housing 32%
- Transportation 18%
- Food 13%
- Personal insurance and pension 11%
- Clothes and related services 4%
- Health care 6%
- All other 16%

Note: "All other" includes expenses such as entertainment, personal care, education, and contributions.

Source: Bureau of Labor Statistics

◆ Practice your skill in reading a circle graph. Fill in the missing information in the chart.

Type of Expense	Housing		Food	Insurance and Pension		
Percentage (%)		18%			6%	4%

Here are the correct answers:

Type of Expense	Housing	Transportation	Food	Insurance and Pension	Health Care	Clothes and Related Services
Percentage (%)	32%	18%	13%	11%	6%	4%

A circle graph gives you a clear picture of what part of the whole each percentage represents. A circle graph also helps you see comparisons. For example, notice that 50% of the average person's budget goes for housing (32%) and transportation (18%).

Strategy: How to Read a Circle Graph

- Read the title. What is the topic of the graph?
- Read the labels on the graph.
- Look at the size of each section. Study the percentages (%). Which portion is largest? Which portion is smallest?
- Notice that the portions add up to 100%.

By law, most divorced fathers must help support their children. Are divorced fathers obeying the law? How are children affected when fathers do not pay child support?

Study the circle graph and answer the questions.

Child Support Payments

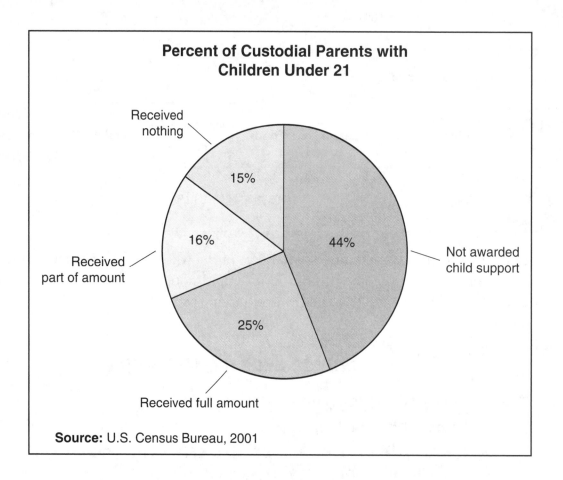

Percent of Custodial Parents with Children Under 21

Received nothing 15%

Received part of amount 16%

Not awarded child support 44%

Received full amount 25%

Source: U.S. Census Bureau, 2001

1. What is the topic of the graph? _____

2. Which section on the graph is the largest? _____

3. Which two sections on the graph are almost the same size?

    _____   _____

4. What does 25% represent?
   (1) single parents who are not awarded child support
   (2) parents who are divorced or separated
   (3) single parents who received the full amount of child support
   (4) single parents who were awarded child support but got nothing

5. What percentage of single parents collected only part of the child support they had been awarded?
   (1) 15%
   (2) 16%
   (3) 25%
   (4) 44%

6. What percentage of single parents received none of the child support they had been awarded?
   (1) 15%
   (2) 16%
   (3) 25%
   (4) 44%

7. What does the graph suggest about single parents who are raising children?
   (1) They usually get support from the other parent.
   (2) Only a small percentage receive all the child support they have been awarded.
   (3) A large percent regret having children.
   (4) Very few are awarded child support.

Check your answers on page 197.

Exercise 2

Developing nations are the world's poorer nations. Most people in these countries make their living by farming. Children get little schooling. There is little medical care. How do you think these nations use the aid that comes to them from richer nations?

Read the passage. Then answer the questions.

Foreign Aid

**Foreign Aid to Developing Nations
by Regions of the World
(in billions of dollars)**

**1990
Total: $24.1 billion**

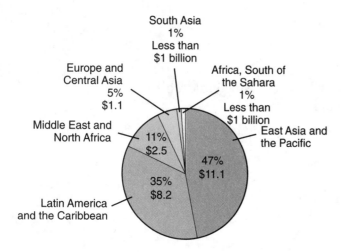

**2006
Total: $280.9 billion**

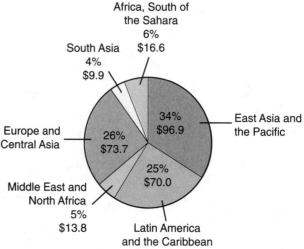

1. Which world region received the second-highest percentage of foreign aid in 1990?
   (1) East Asia and the Pacific
   (2) Latin America and the Caribbean
   (3) Middle East and North America
   (4) Europe and Central Asia

2. What percentage of foreign aid did South Asia receive in 1990?
   (1) 35%
   (2) 11%
   (3) 5%
   (4) 1%

3. Which world region received the lowest percentage of foreign aid in 2006?
   (1) Latin America and the Caribbean
   (2) Middle East and North Africa
   (3) South Asia
   (4) Africa, South of the Sahara

4. On the 2006 graph, how much aid does 6% represent?
   (1) $16.6 billion
   (2) $13.8 billion
   (3) $9.9 billion
   (4) $2.5 billion

5. On the 1990 graph, how much aid does 5% represent?
   (1) $13.8 billion
   (2) $8.2 billion
   (3) $1.1 billion
   (4) less than $1 billion

6. What do the graphs suggest about the foreign aid given to developing nations in 2006?
   (1) All regions received greater percentages of foreign aid in 2006.
   (2) Some regions received smaller percentages of foreign aid in 2006 than in 1990, but other regions received larger percentages.
   (3) All regions received smaller percentages of foreign aid in 2006 than in 1990.
   (4) Only the Middle East and North Africa received a smaller percentage of foreign aid in 2006 than in 1990.

Check your answers on page 197.

Exercise 3

When an employer hires a new worker, the employer pays the worker. What other costs does the employer pay?

Study the circle graph. Then answer the questions.

LANGUAGE Tip

Medical insurance, vacations, holidays, and pensions are called **benefits**. *Bene* means "good." Benefits are the good part of working!

The Cost of Being an Employer

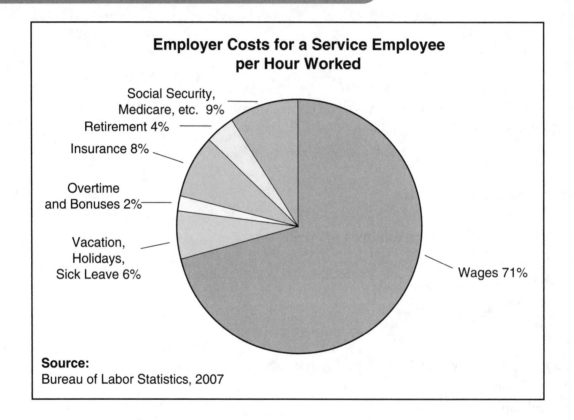

Employer Costs for a Service Employee per Hour Worked

Social Security, Medicare, etc. 9%
Retirement 4%
Insurance 8%
Overtime and Bonuses 2%
Vacation, Holidays, Sick Leave 6%
Wages 71%

Source:
Bureau of Labor Statistics, 2007

1. What percentage of an employer's cost is wages?
   (1) 9%
   (2) 29%
   (3) 71%
   (4) 100%

2. What does 6% represent?
   (1) the employee's wages
   (2) payment for days when the employee did not work
   (3) money put into a retirement account
   (4) taxes paid for the employee

3. What percentage of an employer's cost is insurance, Social Security, and Medicare?
   (1) 4%
   (2) 8%
   (3) 9%
   (4) 17%

4. Which is the smallest cost for an employer?
   (1) overtime and bonuses
   (2) insurance
   (3) vacation, holidays, and sick leave
   (4) retirement

Check your answers on page 197.

Writing Workshop

Prewriting
In this chapter, you studied a circle graph showing how the average American spends money. How do you spend your money each month? What bills do you pay? Make a list of your main expenses. Use this list for ideas.

| rent | food | car insurance | health insurance |
| gas | phone bill | baby supplies | entertainment |

Drafting
Create a two-column chart. Write "Type of Monthly Expense" and "Amount Spent" at the top of the columns. Include the cost of each item on your list.

Now use the list to write a paragraph about your budget. You might explain why one amount is very high or how you would like to change your budget.

Revising
Look at how you have written amounts of money. Use the dollar sign ($), not the word *dollar*. Do not write the cents sign (¢) when you use the dollar sign.

Editing
To make a chart on a computer, open the **Table** menu. Click **Insert** and **Table**. Then decide how many columns and rows you want in your chart.

UNIT 5

Review – Economics

Why do people go to school? What skills are they trying to improve? How will better skills help them? What do these graphs tell you about students?

Study the graphs and answer the questions.

PART A

Education

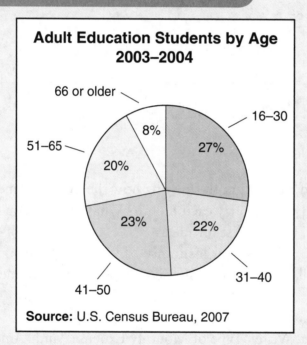

Adult Education Students by Age 2003–2004

66 or older

8%

16–30

27%

51–65

20%

23%

22%

41–50

31–40

Source: U.S. Census Bureau, 2007

1. Which two groups of students are about the same size?
   (1) the youngest and the oldest
   (2) the oldest and those 31–40 years old
   (3) students 16–30 and students 41–50
   (4) students 31–40 and students 41–50

2. In a class of 20 adult education students, how many students are likely to be 16–30 years old?
   (1) 15 students
   (2) 10 students
   (3) 5 students
   (4) 2 students

PART B

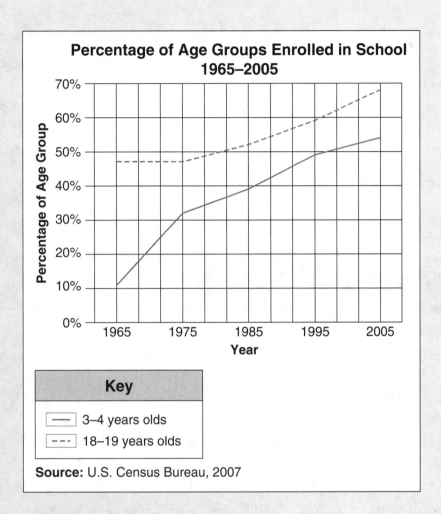

Percentage of Age Groups Enrolled in School
1965–2005

Key

— 3–4 years olds

--- 18–19 years olds

Source: U.S. Census Bureau, 2007

1. What does this line graph show about the percentage of 3–4 year olds who were in school between 1965 and 2005?
   (1) The percentage increased a great deal.
   (2) The percentage dropped sharply.
   (3) The percentage increased and then decreased.
   (4) The percentage remained about the same.

2. What does this line graph show about the percentage of 18–19 year olds who were in school between 1965 and 2005?
   (1) The percentage decreased.
   (2) The percentage increased slowly but steadily.
   (3) The percentage did not change.
   (4) The percentage increased and then decreased.

Check your answers on page 197.

Posttest

This Posttest will help you check how well you have learned the skills that will help you read social studies materials. You should take the Posttest after you have completed all the exercises in this book.

You can check your answers on pages 185–186. Then fill out the Posttest Evaluation Chart on page 184. The chart will tell you which sections of the book you might want to review.

Have you ever loaned or borrowed money? How can loans help people improve?

Read the passage. Then circle the best answer for each question.

Microlending

Microlending is giving tiny (micro) loans to poor people. These people then use the loans to start small businesses. The goal of microloans is to help people help themselves out of poverty.

The idea began in Bangladesh in 1974. Muhammad Yunus is an economist. He tried out his idea with 42 people in one village. Each person was loaned $27 for the purpose of starting a business. He gave people money and told them to pay it back when they could. All of the people repaid their loans.

Dr. Yunus took what he learned and began the Grameen Bank. *Grameen* means "village" in the Bengali language. By 2006, the bank had loaned money to 6 million people. Most people who borrow are women. Loans tend to be for $20 or less, and interest rates are low. This money can help a woman buy cloth so she can make clothing and sell it at the local market. Or it can help someone buy the materials used for making baskets. Then the baskets can be sold for a profit.

Since 1974, Dr. Yunus's idea has grown. Many countries now have microlending programs. In 2006, Dr. Yunus won the Nobel Peace Prize for his work. Those giving the award said that people must "find ways . . . to break out of poverty" if the world is to have lasting peace. Dr. Yunus's idea is one way of helping people move out of poverty.

1. What is the main idea of the passage?
   (1) Microlending programs have been started all over the world.
   (2) Dr. Yunus won the Nobel Peace Prize for his good idea.
   (3) Microlending is one way to help people get out of poverty.
   (4) Dr. Yunus developed microlending to help people out of poverty.

2. Which detail is *not* given in the passage?

   (1) Most loans are $20 or less.
   (2) Interest rates are low.
   (3) A loan for $300 is a large loan.
   (4) Most borrowers are women.

3. Which statement best summarizes Dr. Yunus's idea?

   (1) Giving small loans to poor people helps them start businesses and earn money.
   (2) Low interest rates are an important part of microlending.
   (3) Microlending helps more women than men.
   (4) Microlending in now done in nations all around the world.

4. Which statement best summarizes the quote in paragraph 4 about Dr. Yunus's work?

   (1) Poverty leads to war.
   (2) Having world peace depends on helping people out of poverty.
   (3) Rich people are likely to be peaceful.
   (4) Dr. Yunus's work is one way that people can work themselves out of poverty.

How do you feel when you sit down to fill out your income tax form?

Study the political cartoon and read the background notes. Then answer the questions.

Income Tax

Background notes: Every April, people fill out Form 1040 to report their income to the government. The form asks about a variety of subjects. The form is confusing for some taxpayers. The cartoonist has turned Form 1040 into a maze.

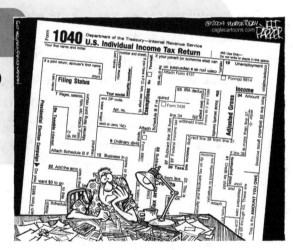

5. Which detail does the cartoonist use to represent how long it can take to fill out Form 1040?

   (1) stacks of papers
   (2) a pencil
   (3) a cup of coffee
   (4) a large desk

6. What inference can you make about how the cartoonist views Form 1040?

   (1) Filling out Form 1040 makes taxpayers happy.
   (2) The 1040 is a puzzle that taxpayers have to work through.
   (3) Filling out Form 1040 is quick and easy.
   (4) Mazes can be scary.

What role did African Americans play in settling the West? What risks did they take to gain freedom?

Read the passage and answer the questions.

African American Pioneers

The word *pioneer* refers to someone who breaks new ground. A pioneer paves new paths for others to follow. This was certainly true for African Americans who went west during the 1800s. The trip west gave them a chance to gain freedom.

One of these pioneers was a man named York. York was born into slavery in Virginia. He was a childhood friend of William Clark. He traveled with Clark on the famous Lewis and Clark expedition. The trip was the first overland journey to the Pacific coast and back. It lasted from 1804 to 1806. York was an important member of the group. He was a good hunter, and once he saved Clark during a flood. As a result of York's bravery, Clark gave York his freedom. Later York became chief of the Crow Indians.

Biddy Mason also found freedom in the West. Her journey began in 1851. She walked from Mississippi to California behind the wagon train of her owner. On the trip, which took a year, she herded cattle, prepared meals, and took care of children. Slavery was against the law in California. With the help of a friend, Mason sued her owner and won her freedom. She settled in Los Angeles and worked as a nurse. In time, she bought land and a building that she rented to businesses. By the late 1860s, Mason was very rich. She became well-known for helping needy people.

These are two of the many forgotten pioneers in history. They escaped slavery in the South and realized their dreams of freedom in the West.

7. According to the passage, what effect did traveling west during the 1800s have for some African Americans?

    (1) sickness and death
    (2) freedom
    (3) adventure
    (4) imprisonment

8. The details in paragraph 2 focus on the experiences of

    (1) Lewis
    (2) Clark
    (3) York
    (4) Crow Indians

9. What happened to Biddy Mason in 1851?

    (1) She left Mississippi, following a wagon train.
    (2) She arrived in California.
    (3) She sued her owner.
    (4) She became a wealthy woman.

10. You can infer from the passage that the most important trait of a pioneer is

    (1) business ability
    (2) knowledge
    (3) courage
    (4) helpfulness

11. Which event happened last to York?

    (1) York won his freedom.
    (2) York was born into slavery in Virginia.
    (3) York became chief of the Crow Indians.
    (4) York acted as a guide on the Lewis and Clark expedition.

12. What happened to Mason as a result of suing her master?

    (1) She won her freedom.
    (2) She owned land.
    (3) She started her own business.
    (4) all of the above

What do today's television viewers expect when they watch political debates? How do TV debates affect what voters think about the candidates? How did TV viewers react to the first TV debate?

Read the passage and answer the questions.

The Kennedy-Nixon Debates

In the fall of 1960, millions of Americans watched the candidates for president talk about important issues. This was the first TV debate in U.S. history.

Senator John F. Kennedy was the Democratic candidate for president. He faced two big problems. The first problem was his age. He was only 43 years old. The second problem was that he had less experience than the Republican candidate, Vice President Richard Nixon. To overcome these problems, Kennedy challenged Nixon to a TV debate. Nixon accepted the challenge. On September 26, the two candidates stood before the TV cameras.

TV viewers noticed differences between these two men right away. Kennedy, wearing a dark suit, looked handsome. He seemed relaxed and full of energy. In contrast, Nixon looked tired and nervous. His suit was the same color as the background, so he looked pale. He refused to wear makeup, and he needed a shave.

Kennedy attacked Nixon right away. He listed Nixon's failures. Nixon defended himself with skill. He talked about his experience in handling Nikita Khrushchev, the leader of the Soviet Union. However, Nixon's remarks did not excite the voters.

During the debate, Nixon looked at Kennedy when speaking. However, Kennedy spoke directly to the TV viewers. This is one reason viewers thought Kennedy was the winner of the debate.

Later the Democrats used scenes from the debate in an advertisement. It showed Kennedy answering questions with great confidence. Then it showed Nixon's reaction. He was sweating and frowning.

The polls predicted a very close election. This prediction came true. Some political experts believed that the first TV debate was the reason that Kennedy won the election. Kennedy agreed with their opinion. He said, "We wouldn't have had a prayer without [television]."

13. How did Kennedy solve his problems as a Democratic candidate for president?

   (1) He got TV stars to say they would vote for him.
   (2) He challenged Nixon to a TV debate.
   (3) He asked political experts for their opinions.
   (4) He listed Nixon's failures as vice president.

14. Which difference between Kennedy and Nixon made TV viewers think that Kennedy won the debate?

   (1) Kennedy was more handsome.
   (2) Kennedy appeared more relaxed.
   (3) Kennedy was full of energy.
   (4) Kennedy spoke directly to the TV viewers.

15. According to the passage, which was an opinion of political experts?

   (1) Kennedy was too young to be a good president.
   (2) Nixon had experience with the leader of the Soviet Union.
   (3) The TV debate was the reason for Kennedy's victory.
   (4) Nixon skillfully defended Kennedy's attacks.

16. From the information in the passage, you might predict that

   (1) candidates will work hard to prepare themselves for TV debates
   (2) Democratic candidates for president will keep winning TV debates
   (3) Republican candidates for president will improve their debating skills
   (4) elections for president will continue to be very close races

17. According to the passage, which two factors did Kennedy have to overcome during this TV debate with Nixon?

   (1) his lack of ease and his unattractive image
   (2) his tendency to sweat and frown
   (3) his youth and his lack of experience
   (4) his unexciting delivery and his lack of ability to look his opponent in the eye

18. From the description of how Nixon and Kennedy performed in the TV debate, you might predict that

   (1) Nixon would win the debate
   (2) the two candidates' performances would be considered equal
   (3) Kennedy would win the debate
   (4) none of the above

Where did the United States fight battles with Mexico during the Mexican War? What paths did U.S. troops take during that time?

Use the map and the background notes to answer the questions.

The Mexican War

Background notes: From 1846 to 1848, the United States and Mexico fought a war. At the end of the war, the United States paid Mexico 15 million dollars for a large area of land that stretched from Texas to the Pacific Ocean. General Zachary Taylor, Colonel Philip Kearny, and General Winfield Scott were the leaders of the U.S. troops. This map shows the movement of their troops. It also shows the locations of U.S. and Mexican victories.

Important Battles in the Mexican War
(1846–1848)

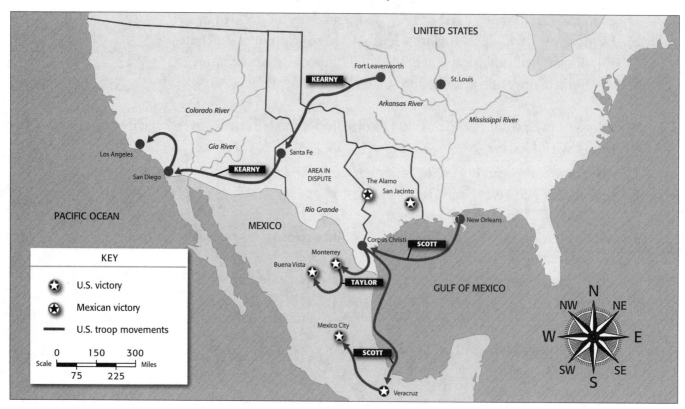

19. In which of these places was there a Mexican victory?

    (1) Santa Fe
    (2) Buena Vista
    (3) the Alamo
    (4) San Jacinto

20. In which direction did Colonel Kearny's troops move after they stopped at Santa Fe?

    (1) northwest
    (2) southwest
    (3) east
    (4) west

21. About how many miles did General Scott's troops travel from Veracruz to Mexico City?

    (1) about 75 miles
    (2) about 150 miles
    (3) about 225 miles
    (4) over 300 miles

22. Where did Zachary Taylor's troops go right after they left Corpus Christi?

    (1) Monterrey
    (2) New Orleans
    (3) Mexico City
    (4) Buena Vista

23. According to the map, which country had more victories during the Mexican War—the United States or Mexico?

    _____

24. About how many miles is Fort Leavenworth from Santa Fe?

    (1) 200 miles
    (2) 100 miles
    (3) 300 miles
    (4) 500 miles

These graphs give information about the marriage rates and birth rates in the United States. Do these two graphs show similar patterns? Or do they show different patterns?

Study the line graphs and answer the questions.

Marriage and Birth Rates

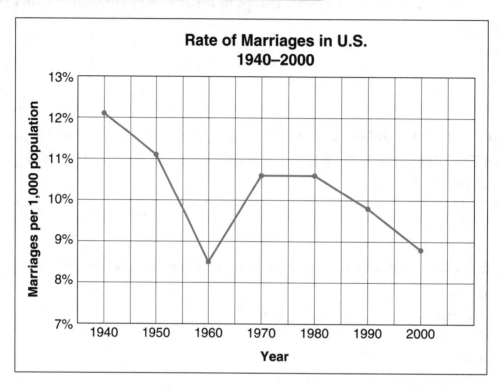

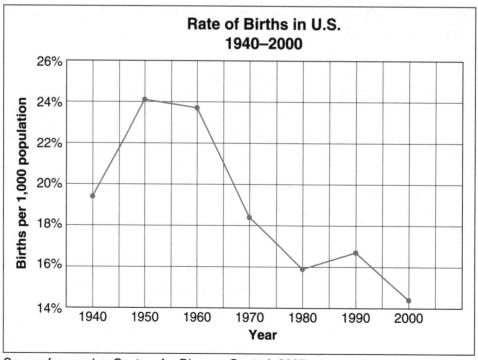

Source for graphs: Centers for Disease Control, 2007

25. During which period of time did marriage rates remain unchanged?

    (1) from 1940 to 1950

    (2) from 1960 to 1970

    (3) from 1970 to 1980

    (4) from 1990 to 2000

26. What was the rate of birth in 1980?

    (1) 14%

    (2) 16%

    (3) 17%

    (4) 18%

27. During which period of time did the greatest decrease of births occur?

    (1) from 1940 to 1950

    (2) from 1960 to 1970

    (3) from 1970 to 1980

    (4) from 1990 to 2000

28. What trend do the two line graphs show about the period from 1990 to 2000?

    (1) a drop in both the number of marriages and the number of births

    (2) a decrease in marriages and an increase in births

    (3) an increase in marriages and a decrease in births

    (4) a steady increase in both the number of marriages and the number of births

29. From 1980 to 1990, the rate of births increased and the rate of marriages

    (1) stayed the same

    (2) decreased

    (3) increased

    (4) went up and then down

30. Which fact do you learn from reading the second chart?

    (1) The rate of births generally decreased from 1950 to 2000.

    (2) The rate of births generally increased from 1970 to 2000.

    (3) The rate of births changed little from 1950 to 1980.

    (4) The rate of births changes a great deal every ten years.

Check your answers on pages 185–186.

Posttest Evaluation Chart

Use the Postttest Answer Key on pages 185–186 to check your answers. Next, find the number of each question you missed. Circle that number in the Item Number column of this chart. Then write the number of correct answers you had for each skill. If you need more practice in any skill, refer to the chapter that covers that skill.

Chapter	Skill	Item Number	Number Correct
1	Finding the Main Idea	1, 8	
2	Finding Details	2, 17	
3	Summarizing	3, 4	
5	Sequence	9, 11	
6	Cause and Effect	7, 12	
7	Problem and Solution	13	
8	Comparison and Contrast	14, 29	
9	Fact and Opinion	15, 30	
10	Inferences	10	
11	Predicting	16, 18	
12	Political Cartoons	5, 6	
13	Map Keys	19, 22, 23	
14	Finding Direction and Distances	20, 21, 24	
17	Line Graphs	25, 26, 27, 28	

Posttest Answer Key

1. **(4)** The passage discusses Dr. Yunus's idea of microlending.

2. **(3)** The passage mentions only small loans.

3. **(1)** This is the only sentence that states the main idea and the most important points of the passage. Each of the other sentences states just one fact about microlending.

4. **(2)** This is only answer choice that includes the words *peace* and *poverty*.

5. **(3)** The cup of coffee gives the idea that filling out the form takes time. The man needs coffee to stay awake.

6. **(2)** A maze is a puzzle. You can infer that the cartoonist thinks filling out a tax form is like putting together a puzzle.

7. **(2)** The last sentence of paragraph 1 states that some African Americans were given their freedom after they traveled to the West.

8. **(3)** The details of paragraph 2 support the topic sentence "One of these pioneers was a man named York."

9. **(1)** The beginning of paragraph 3 explains what Biddy Mason did in 1851.

10. **(3)** Clues that support this inference include the word "bravery" in paragraph 2.

11. **(3)** York became a chief of the Crow Indians after he was born into slavery (2), acted as guide on the Lewis and Clark expedition (4), and won his freedom (1).

12. **(4)** As a result of suing her owner, Mason won her freedom (1), owned land (2), and started her own business (3).

13. **(2)** Sentence 6 in paragraph 2 states Kennedy's solution to his problems.

14. **(4)** Paragraph 5 explains this key difference between Kennedy and Nixon in the TV debates.

15. **(3)** The last paragraph states that this was the opinion of political experts.

16. **(1)** Kennedy probably won the election because of his success in the TV debate. You can infer that candidates since then have spent long hours preparing for these debates.

17. **(3)** Choices (1), (2), and (4) are factors that affected Nixon, not Kennedy, during the TV debate.

18. **(3)** Kennedy's ease in front of a camera, his energy, and his ability to speak directly to viewers would lead to the prediction that Kennedy would win the debate.

19. **(3)** The symbol next to the Alamo means "Mexican victory."

20. **(2)** The arrow on the map points left and down, which is to the southwest (SW).

21. **(3)** According to the map scale, the distance is about 225 miles.

22. **(1)** The arrow on the map shows Taylor's troops went from Corpus Christi to Monterrey.

23. The United States; the map shows five U.S. victories but only one Mexican victory.

24. (4) According to the map, the distance is a little more than 500 miles.

25. (3) The line between the years 1970 and 1980 goes straight across. This shows that the marriage rate for this time period did not change.

26. (2) The point on the line graph for 1980 is nearly 16%.

27. (2) The line on the graph goes down the fastest from 1960 (about 24%) to 1970 (about 18%).

28. (1) On both graphs, the line drops between 1990 and 2000.

29. (2) The rate of marriages decreased between 1980 and 1990.

30. (1) According to the graph, the rate of births went down from 1950 to 2000, except for a small rise from 1980 to 1990.

Answer Key

Unit 1: World History

Chapter 1: Finding the Main Idea

Exercise 1, pages 6-7

1. (2) The passage describes the causes of the revolution. The other answer choices describe just one cause.
2. (2) Sentence 2 states the main idea. Each paragraph in the passage describes one cause of the revolution. Answer choices (1) and (3) describe the results of the revolution. Answer choice (4) only lists one cause.
3. (1) The other sentences in the paragraph add information that explains this sentence.
4. (4) The best answer gives a general explanation. The other answer choices give only one reason why the nobles and clergy were hated.
5. (3) Paragraphs 3 and 4 state this information.

Exercise 2, pages 8-9

1. (3) The passage describes the discovery of a vaccine against smallpox. Each of the other answer choices is the topic of just one part of the passage.
2. (1) Sentence 1 states the main idea. Each paragraph in the passage adds information that explains the main idea.
3. (4) The definition of *immune* can be figured out from context clues in sentence 2 of paragraph 5.
4. (2) The other sentences in the paragraph explain information in this sentence.
5. (3) This is the only answer that pulls all the information in the paragraph into one statement. The other answer choices state only some of the information.
6. (1) The other sentences in the paragraph explain information in this sentence by giving examples.

Exercise 3, pages 10-11

1. (4) The passage is about Shah Jahan, why he built the Taj Mahal, and what the Taj Mahal looks like.
2. (1) The other sentences in the paragraph give details to explain this sentence.
3. (3) The paragraph is about the marriage of Shah Jahan and Mumtaz Mahal.

Chapter 2: Finding Details

Exercise 1, pages 14-15

Answers may vary. Use these answers as a guideline.

1. in Europe and Asia; it was made up of Russia, 19 republics, and several smaller regions
2. Only members of the Communist Party could run for office or hold government jobs.
3. It was difficult to get groceries, fuel, consumer goods, and housing.
4. Mikhail Gorbachev
5. Gorbachev saw that the people were angry about how the country was being run.
6. 1991

Exercise 2, pages 16-17

1. (3) From the time Columbus arrived in the Americas, food was traded between Europeans and Native Americans.
2. (2) This was the exchange (or trade) of foods and animals from one continent to another.
3. (1) The Columbian Exchange began when Columbus arrived in the Americas in 1492. Explorers in the 1500s continued to find new foods in the Americas and to take foods to the Americas.
4. (1) Sugarcane was brought to the Americas by Europeans, but it had originally come from Asia.
5. (4) Europeans took these new foods to Asia when they went to Asia to buy spices and other goods.

6. (3) The last paragraph says that Native Americans died when they caught diseases from the Europeans.

Exercise 3, pages 18-19

Answers may vary. Use these answers as a guideline.
1. in Great Britain
2. Farm workers did a variety of tasks outdoors, but factory workers worked inside and did the same jobs every day.
3. in 1800
4. mostly women and children
5. They were afraid they would be fired.
6. Workers worked 12 to 16 hours a day, six days a week.

Chapter 3: Summarizing

Exercise 1, pages 22-23

1. (3) This is the only idea that relates to all the details in the passage.
2. (2) Answer choices (1), (3), and (4) are true, but they do not restate the main idea and the important details of the paragraph.
3. (2) The context tells you that *backward* has to do with time.
4. (a), (d), and (e) are mentioned in the passage. Answers (b) and (c) are not.
5. (4) This statement mentions all the important details of the passage.

Exercise 2, pages 24-25

1. (1) This is the only answer choice that pulls all the details together.
2. (2) This is the only answer choice that makes a general statement that includes all the important details.
3. (1) This summary contains all of the important details in the paragraph.
4. (3) This information is stated in paragraph 1.
5. (1) The meaning of the word is interesting, but it does not need to be included in a summary.

Exercise 3, pages 26-27

Answers may vary. Use these answers as a guideline.
1. Confucianism was based on five relationships: ruler and ruled, parent and child, husband and wife, older and younger brothers, and friend and friend. Except between friend and friend, the second person was less important.
2. Respect, loyalty, and obedience were duties of the less important person. Caring for the less important person was the duty of the superior person.

Chapter 4: Reading Photographs and Paintings

Exercise 1, pages 30-31

Answers will vary. Use these answers as a guideline.
1. They are cheering, smiling, and waving.
2. He is a candidate. Perhaps he is Mugabe.
3. They look like middle-class or poor people.
4. The photographer wanted to show that the people were happy to be taking part in the elections.
5. Many people are probably hoping they will have new leaders who can help them solve their problems.

Exercise 2, pages 32-33

Answers will vary. Use the following as a guideline.
1. the rise and fall of Napoleon Bonaparte
2. the rock on the ground with the name *Bonaparte* written on it
3. (2) The caption gives a hint. It says he is at the "peak of his power," so he must be in control.
4. (3) His arm is raised, and his hand is pointing forward. As the nation's leader, he is pointing the way for others to follow.

Exercise 3, pages 34-35

1. (3) The passage describes the development and training of the samurai class. Answer (1) is not discussed. Answer choices (3) and (4) each describe just one detail in the passage.

2. (2) The last two sentences of paragraph 2 tell you this answer.

3. (4) The last sentence of the passage gives the answer.

4. (1) The faces on the warriors look fierce. The samurai who is on the ground is still fighting.

Unit 1 Review—World History, pages 36–37

1. (4) The paragraph discusses how the Communists tried to control the nation's economy.

2. (2) The photo shows motorbikes, and the passage mentions that motorbikes are an important import.

3. (3) The other items are sold; that is, they are exported.

4. (4) The paragraph describes how the modern country of Vietnam was formed.

5. (3) Paragraph 3 gives this information.

Unit 2: U.S. History

Chapter 5: Sequence

Exercise 1, pages 42–43

Answers may vary. Use these answers as a guideline.

1. **December 17, 1903**
   Wright brothers fly first successful plane
   May 20, 1927
   Charles Lindbergh's nonstop solo flight across the Atlantic Ocean
   May 20, 1932
   Amelia Earhart's nonstop solo flight across the Atlantic Ocean

2. Like Lindbergh, "Lucky Lindy," Earhart made a nonstop solo flight across the Atlantic Ocean.

3. It was the first successful airplane flight.

Exercise 2, pages 44–45

1. 1781
2. 1770
3. 1769
4. 1817

5. 1771

6.

```
|——|—|—|————————————|———————————————|
 1769 1770 1771        1781            1817
San Diego  Monterey  San Luis    Los Angeles  Last mission
built.     built.    Obespo built. founded.    built.
```

Answers may vary. Use these answers as a guideline.

7. Spain decided to settle California because Russia was showing interest in the area.

8. A mission had a church, a house for the priest, houses and workshops for Native Americans, orchards, and barns.

Exercise 3, pages 46–47

Correct order: 3, 2, 4, 6, 1, 5.

Chapter 6: Cause and Effect

Exercise 1, pages 50–51

PART A

1. (2) The working conditions are described in paragraph 2. These conditions made factory workers angry.

2. (1) The topic sentence is the first sentence of the paragraph. It states the cause (workers were unhappy) and the effect (labor unions began to grow).

3. (4) Sentence 6 of the last paragraph states this effect. The sentence begins with the clue words *as a result*.

PART B

1. 60 hours × $ .25 = $15 per week
2. (a) dirty; (b) unsafe; (c) overcrowded

Exercise 2, pages 52–53

PART A

1. cause, effect
2. cause, effect
3. effect, cause
4. cause, effect
5. effect, cause

PART B

1. (3) The last three paragraphs of the passage give details explaining why the West was so wild.

2. (4) The last sentence of paragraph 3 explains why Jesse James was so violent.

Exercise 3, pages 54–55

PART A

1. (3) The first sentence of the passage states the topic of the passage: the effects of cars.
2. (2) The first sentence of paragraph 2 states that farmers drove regularly to the city because they had more roads to drive on.
3. (4) Paragraph 3 states this negative effect.

PART B

Answers may vary. Use these answers as a guideline.

Good Effects
(1) roads connected city and country
(2) people could take long trips
(3) tourism grew

Bad Effects
(1) car accidents
(2) traffic jams and street noise
(3) sexual looseness
(4) "getaway" cars

Chapter 7: Problem and Solution

Exercise 1, pages 58–59

1. (4) Sentence 1 in paragraph 3 states the problem.
2. (3) Sentence 3 in paragraph 4 states the results of the first Earth Day.
3. (3) The last sentence in paragraph 4 states the effect that Earth Day had on Congress.

Exercise 2, pages 60–61

Answers may vary. Use these answers as a guideline.
1. cotton
2. The Cherokee occupied land where cotton could be grown.
3. The law required Native Americans to give up their land. In exchange, they were given new land west of the Mississippi.
4. President Jackson thought the law was a fair solution to a difficult problem. He believed the Cherokee would have better lives.
5. The Cherokee refused to leave Georgia.
6. The "Trail of Tears" was the forced march of the Cherokee toward Oklahoma. About 4,000 Cherokee died along the way.

Exercise 3, pages 62–63

1. T The first two sentences of the passage state this information.
2. F The first problem Roosevelt set out to solve was the banking problem (paragraph 2, sentence 2)
3. F During the "bank holiday," the banks were closed for four days (paragraph 2, sentence 4).
4. T Paragraph 2 explains the Emergency Banking Act.
5. T This statement restates Roosevelt's first quotation in paragraph 3.
6. F When the banks reopened, people deposited their savings in them (paragraph 3, last sentence).
7. F Roosevelt admitted that his solutions might not always work (end of paragraph 4).

Chapter 8: Comparison and Contrast

Exercise 1, pages 66–67

Answers may vary. Use these answers as a guideline.

	Rosie the Riveter	Condoleezza Rice
1.	1940s, during World War II	beginning in 2005
2.	overalls	business suits
3.	factory	private jet, around the world
4.	building war planes, navy ships, and army tanks	meeting with presidents and prime ministers
5.	to bring freedom	to bring freedom

Exercise 2, pages 68–69

PART A

1. F The newspaper article praised Lincoln for the way he was leading the nation (paragraph 2, sentence 3).
2. F The beginning of paragraph 5 states that Lincoln might not be elected today.
3. T Paragraph 5 makes this statement.

4. F The Bible was Lincoln's source of strength (paragraph 4, sentence 2). Newspapers usually criticized him.

5. T The last paragraph makes this point.

PART B
(3) The cartoon artist wants people to understand that Lincoln might not be elected today because he was not handsome or polished.

Exercise 3, pages 70-71
1. (2) The first sentence states that both Washington and DuBois shared this concern.

2. (1) Sentence 4 in paragraph 3 makes this comparison.

3. (3) The first sentence of the last paragraph states this difference.

Unit 2 Review—U.S. History, pages 72-73
1. (2) The first sentence in the passage says that Pearl Harbor was bombed on December 7, 1941. The second sentence states that war was declared "the next day." That date was December 8, 1941.

2. (3) Sentence 2 in paragraph 3 states the problem.

3. (4) The last sentence in the passage states the differences.

4. (2) The last two sentences in paragraph 1 describe what the Japanese and Japanese Americans had to leave behind. The other answer choices describe what the camps were like, not how the people were affected by them.

Unit 3: Civics and Government

Chapter 9: Fact and Opinion

Exercise 1, pages 78-79

PART A
1. F Paragraph 1 explains that delegates met in 1787 to write a new plan for government.

2. F Paragraphs 3–5 describe some of the compromises.

3. O This was the opinion of large states, but small states did not agree with this idea.

4. F This statement is proved by information in paragraph 4.

5. F This information is stated in paragraph 5.

6. O Many people might agree with this statement. However, the words "not a good solution" tell you that this statement is an opinion.

PART B
(1), (2), (5) These statements can be proved by information in the passage. Statements (3), (4), and (6) are opinions.

Exercise 2, pages 80-81
1. (3) Not everyone would agree with this statement.

2. (2) Paragraph 3 explains why bloggers write their ideas on the Internet. Notice that answer choice (3) is a fact. It can be proved.

3. (2) This statement cannot be proved true. Some people think other ways work better.

4. (4) The last paragraph explains that putting out news quickly may not be the best way to spread accurate information.

Exercise 3, pages 82-83
1. F Paragraph 1 lists only four requirements.

2. O Many people agree with this idea, but it is an opinion.

3. O This statement cannot be proved. The word *only* is a clue that this could be an opinion.

4. O This statement cannot be proved.

5. F Details in the passage about how women were treated help prove this statement.

6. F This passage explains that many people did use this argument.

Chapter 10: Inferences

Exercise 1, pages 86-87

1. (3) The passage suggests that the writer thinks that all political campaigns are important. The last sentence provides the most important clue.
2. (4) Paragraphs 3 and 4 discuss the jobs that volunteers do. Putting on address labels requires different skills than talking to people on the phone or driving voters to the polls.
3. (2) The information in paragraph 3 helps you figure out why the scripts are important. The other answer choices are not suggested.
4. (2) The opening sentences in paragraphs 2 and 3 are clues to this answer.
5. (1), (2), and (4) are jobs for volunteers. Choices (3) and (5) are jobs usually done by paid campaign workers.

Exercise 2, pages 88-89

1. (4) The passage provides examples of tax dollars paying for public services.
2. (2) The writer lists many important services that taxes pay for.
3. (3) Federal tax money is usually used for programs that help people all over the United States.
4. (2), (3), and (5). Choices (1) and (4) would be paid for by city taxes.

Exercise 3, pages 90-91

1. To protect this right, "sunshine laws" have been written (the first sentence in paragraph 2).
2. Florida's sunshine law is a good example (sentence 3 in paragraph 3).
3. (Answers will vary.) Sunshine laws make sure that public officials cannot hide what they do.

Chapter 11: Predicting

Exercise 1, pages 94-95

Answers will vary. Use these answers as a guideline.

1. The U.S. Supreme Court said that all schools had to be desegregated.
2. They predicted it would not be easy.
3. One of the following: Some districts allowed private schools to open for white students only. Some districts refused to obey. By 1969, the Supreme Court ruled that segregated schools had to end immediately.
4. The education they received was better than it was before schools were desegregated.

Exercise 2, pages 96-97

1. (4) Sentence 3 in paragraph 5 states that family is the most important factor.
2. (2) Women and people who live in big cities tend to be Democrats. This information is in paragraphs 3 and 4.
3. (1) You can make this prediction from information in the first sentence in paragraph 3.
4. (3) You can infer this from the information in paragraph 6.
5. (3) The information in the last sentence of the passage gives evidence to support this prediction.

Exercise 3, pages 98-99

Answers will vary. Use these answers as a guideline.

1. because the president does not agree with the bill passed by Congress
2. by two-thirds of Congress voting to pass the bill again
3. More than two-thirds of Congress had voted for the bill the first time.
4. The president does nothing with the bill. It does not become law because Congress is not meeting, so it cannot pass the bill again.

Chapter 12: Political Cartoons

Exercise 1, pages 102-103

Answers will vary. Use these answers as a guideline.

1. Some people believe if costs were controlled, more Americans could afford health care.
2. They cannot afford medical insurance.
3. poor people who need health care
4. decreases, reductions
5. They have removed its wheels.
6. He is left helpless.
7. Poor people will suffer. They will not have money to pay for medical treatment.

Exercise 2, pages 104-105

Answers may vary. Use these answers as a guideline.

1. Clinton and Obama
2. public financing
3. Senator Clinton is driving one truck, and Senator Obama is driving the other. The man in the car represents the public.
4. Money is blowing around because the tops of the trucks are open. This means there is no limit to the money candidates can raise.
5. The closed container means there is a limit to the amount of public financing.
6. The car may be smashed by the two trucks.
7. The cartoonist disapproves. Smashing the car means that the public will be hurt when so much money is raised by the candidates for their campaigns.

Exercise 3, pages 106-107

Answers will vary. Use these answers as a guideline.

1. It means that there are two choices and neither choice is a good one.
2. One is Israel, and the other is HAMAS.
3. The dove and the olive branch are caught. This means that peace is caught between two sides that refuse to change their ideas.
4. The cartoonist does not think there is any chance for peace in the Middle East.

Unit 3 Review—Civics and Government, pages 108-109

PART A

1. (3) Paragraph 5 says that many nations are trying to make changes to slow down global warming.
2. (1) Paragraph 4, sentence 3 says that scientists predict this will happen. Predictions are always opinions.
3. (2) Paragraphs 2, 3, and 4 describe changes that will affect both humans and animals.

PART B

1. (2) The need for sunglasses symbolizes the need for polar bears to protect themselves from the Sun.
2. (3) Polar bears need ice. The cartoon is suggesting that polar bears will have to look for ice somewhere else if the polar ice cap melts.

Unit 4: Geography

Chapter 13: Map Keys

Exercise 1, pages 114-115

1. Chicago, Dallas, Denver, Rapid City
2. Los Angeles, San Francisco, Minneapolis, New York, Miami
3. Atlanta, Seattle
4. Minneapolis, Rapid City, Seattle
5. 77°
6. 95°
7. Denver
8. Answers will vary.

Exercise 2, pages 116-117

1. (2) The area of central Mexico shows the highest population density.
2. (3) People like to live in areas that have a nice climate.
3. (4) Panama's highest population density is only 25–129 persons per square mile.
4. (3) Most of Honduras and Nicaragua have 25–129 persons per square mile.

5. (4) This area has an average of 0–24 persons per square mile.
6. (3) Belize has a population density of 25–129 persons per square mile.

Exercise 3, pages 118-119

1. (1) The map shows that about one-fourth of Arizona is covered by federal reservations for Native Americans.
2. (1) A circle on the map represents Native American groups living outside the reservations. Oregon has three circles. The other choices have more circles.
3. (3) A triangle represents state reservations. New York has the most triangles.

Chapter 14: Finding Directions and Distances

Exercise 1, pages 122-123

1. Texas (TX)
2. north
3. about 1,300 miles
4. about 500 miles
5. Connecticut (CT), Maine (ME), Rhode Island (RI)
6. about 1,700 miles
7. Florida (FL)
8. California(CA), Illinois (IL), North Carolina (NC), Oklahoma (OK), Pennsylvania (PA)

Exercise 2, pages 124-125

1. (2) The map shows the wet monsoons blowing toward the northeast.
2. (4) The map shows the dry monsoons blowing toward the southwest.
3. (3) China is northeast of India.
4. (4) Pakistan is west of India.
5. 800 miles
6. 1,000 miles
7. 700 miles

Exercise 3, pages 126-127

1. south, west
2. west, south
3. Virginia, North Carolina, South Carolina, Georgia, Tennessee, Alabama, Mississippi, Louisiana
4. 225 miles

5. 175 miles
6. 400 miles
7. 275 miles

Chapter 15: Historical Maps

Exercise 1, pages 130-131

Answers to questions 1 and 2 may vary. Use these answers as a guideline.

1. women's suffrage in 1914 *or* when women gained the right to vote
2. to add an amendment to the Constitution that would give women the right to vote
3. (a) Arizona (AZ), California (CA), Colorado (CO), Idaho (ID), Kansas (KS), Montana (MT), Nevada (NV), Oregon (OR), Utah (UT), Washington (WA), Wyoming (WY)
   (b) in the west
4. Illinois (IL)
5. List any six of the following: Alabama (AL), Arkansas (AR), Delaware (DE), Florida (FL), Georgia (GA), Indiana (IN), Maine (ME), Maryland (MD), Missouri (MO), North Carolina (NC), Pennsylvania (PA), South Carolina (SC), Tennessee (TN), Texas (TX), Virginia (VA), West Virginia (WV)

Exercise 2, pages 132-133

1. 15
2. France, Great Britain, Italy
3. Union of South Africa
4. Ethiopia and Liberia
5. France
6. about 4,000 miles
7. French Equatorial Africa and French West Africa
8. north Africa

Exercise 3, pages 134-135

1. 19
2. 3
3. Monterey
4. Any two of the following: San Diego, San Francisco, San Jose
5. about 200 miles
6. about 75 miles

Unit 4 Review–Geography, pages 136-137

1. (4) The Goodnight-Loving Trail ran from San Antonio, Texas, to Cheyenne, Wyoming.
2. (1) The railroad line on the California coast is the Southern Pacific.
3. (4) Using the map scale, you can estimate that the distance is about 500 miles.
4. (2) The map shows three railroad lines leading to and from Chicago.
5. (3) The map shows that San Antonio was connected to four cattle trails.
6. (1) The Shawnee Trail ended in Kansas City.

Unit 5: Economics

Chapter 16: Charts

Exercise 1, pages 142-143

1. F Less than half (45%) of workers want strong unions.
2. T 78% of workers are happy with their benefits. Benefits include vacations, pension, holidays, and insurance.
3. F Since 70% of workers work day shifts, only about 30% of workers work night shifts.
4. T 56% of workers feel they are fairly paid. This is a little more than half of all workers.
5. T 88% of workers are proud of the companies they work for.
6. T Only 17% of workers have more than one job. This is about one in every six workers.
7. F 54% of workers have flexible hours if they need them. Therefore, more than half of all workers could probably go to a doctor's appointment during the day.
8. T 53% is about half.
9. F Only 36% (about one-third) of workers have three or more good friends at their jobs.
10. F Since 39% percent of the workers in this survey have worked two years or less at their currents jobs, you cannot infer that most workers plan to keep their current jobs for a long time.
11. F A little more than half (57%) of workers work in teams.
12. T 85% of workers are learning on the job. This is a very high percentage.

Exercise 2, pages 144-145

1. Brazil (190 million people)
2. Peru (53%)
3. Brazil, Mexico, Panama, Peru
4. Costa Rica
5. Peru
6. Costa Rica ($12,500)
7. Peru ($6,600)
8. Mexico (3.2%)
9. lower
10. Brazil and Peru
11. Yes. Mexico has an unemployment rate of 3.2%. Only 18% of people in Mexico live below the poverty line.
12. Brazil. Half of Brazil's population is 95 million people. The number of possible workers in the country is 97.8 million. This is more than half of Brazil's population.

Exercise 3, pages 146-147

1. $20,000,000
2. Shaquille O'Neal
3. Allen Iverson and Stephon Marbury
4. Allen Iverson and Stephon Marbury
5. Kevin Garnett
6. $21,600,000
7. New York Yankees
8. Todd Helton
9. Alex Rodriguez, Jason Giambi, and Derek Jeter
10. Alex Rodriguez

Chapter 17: Line Graphs

Exercise 1, pages 150-151

PART A
1. 1947 to 2004
2. the percentage of women aged 16 or older in the workforce
3. The percentage of working women grew from 1947 until about 1990. Since 1990, the percentage has stayed about the same.
4. 40%
5. 1990
6. 1970 to 1990; the rate grew from about 43% to about 58%
7. 20%; 1947 was about 35%, and 2004 was about 55%

PART B
1. (2) In 1980, about 50% of women were in the workforce.
2. (4) About 50% of women were working in 1980, and almost 60% were working in 2000.
3. (3)

Exercise 2, pages 152-153
1. (2) Iran and Iraq each produced about 3 million barrels per day in 1990.
2. (3) Iraq's greatest decline began after 1990. (The Gulf War was fought in January and February of 1991.)
3. (4) Iran produced about 4 million barrels a day in 2005.
4. (4) Iraq produced much less oil in 1995 than in 1990. Iran and Venezuela increased their production during this period.
5. (3) Venezuela produced about 2.8 million barrels per day in 2000.
6. (1) The line graph shows many ups and downs in Iraq's oil production.

Exercise 3, pages 154-155
1. (2) In 1970, the income and spending were about equal.

2. (1) The biggest drop in spending occurred in 1946, just after World War II.
3. (4) There was a brief time from 1999 to 2001 that the government spent less money than it received.
4. (3) During the 1960s, spending and income were about equal.
5. (1) Spending too much money cannot continue. The government must reduce the amount it spends, or it must collect more taxes.

Chapter 18: Bar Graphs

Exercise 1, pages 158-159
1. deaths due to work injuries, from 1992 through 2006
2. number of deaths
3. about 6,600 deaths
4. 2004 and 2006; about 5,700 workers died each year
5. From 1994 through 2002, the numbers decreased.
6. 2002
7. about 200 more deaths
8. (3) The government, labor unions, and employers are all trying hard to keep workers safe on the job.

Exercise 2, pages 160-161
1. (3) The United States bought the most imports from Japan (about $150 million worth of goods).
2. (1) The bar graph shows that the difference is the smallest for Belgium (about $5 million worth of goods).
3. (4) Japan bought much more than any other nation (about $60 million worth of goods).
4. (1) France bought a little more than $20 million of U.S. products.
5. (4) Ireland and Venezuela each bought about $10 million worth of U.S. goods.
6. (3) The key and the title of the graph tell this answer.

Exercise 3, pages 162-163

1. (3) The firefighter is the highest-paid worker on the graph.
2. (4) A firefighter earned about $20 per hour in 2006. This is about twice as much as a cook, who earned only about $10.
3. (4) The average bus driver and the average firefighter increased their wages the most.
4. (2) The wages of all the workers on this chart increased between 2004 and 2006. Therefore, it is logical to infer that most workers' wages are increased year by year. The information mentioned in the other answer choices is not given on the graph.

Chapter 19: Circle Graphs

Exercise 1, pages 166-167

1. child support payments
2. Not awarded child support
3. Received part of amount and Received nothing
4. (3) 25% of parents who were awarded child support received the full amount.
5. (2) 16% did not receive the full child support that had been awarded to them.
6. (1) 15% did not receive any of the child support payments that should have been sent to them.
7. (2) The graph shows that only 25% percent of single parents receive full child support payments. Most single parents are not awarded child support, do not receive payments, or receive only part of the payments.

Exercise 2, pages 168-169

1. (2) Latin America and the Caribbean received 35 percent of the foreign aid given in 1990. This is a little less than the percentage of aid sent to East Asia and the Pacific.
2. (4) South Asia received 1 percent in 1990.

3. (3) South Asia received the lowest percentage (4%) of aid in 2006.
4. (1) The graph shows that 6% represents $16.6 billion.
5. (3) The graph shows that 5% represents $1.1 billion.
6. (2) The two graphs show that East Asia and the Pacific, Latin America and the Caribbean, and the Middle East and North Africa received smaller percentages in 2006. The other three regions received larger percentages. Notice, however, that each region received more money because the total amount of foreign aid was larger in 2006 than in 1990.

Exercise 3, pages 170-171

1. (3) 71%
2. (2) 6% represents the money employers must pay their workers for days they are sick, on vacation, or having holidays.
3. (4) 17%; this is 8% for insurance and 9% for Social Security and Medicare.
4. (1) Overtime and bonuses are only about 2% of employee costs.

Unit 5 Review—Economics, pages 172-173

PART A

1. (4) 22% of adult education students are ages 31–40; 23% of adult education students are ages 41–50.
2. (3) 27% (students ages 16–30) is about one-fourth. One-fourth of 20 students is five students, so about 5 students are age 30 or younger.

PART B

1. (1) The percentage of 3–4 year olds that attend school has increased each year since 1965.
2. (2) Although the change has not been great, the percentage continues to increase.